THE MAGIC OF Seeds

THE NATURE-LOVER'S GUIDE TO GROWING GARDEN FLOWERS AND HERBS FROM SEED

Clare Gogerty

DAVID & CHARLES

www.davidandcharles.com

Contents

Discovering seeds

There is something poetic about seeds: they arrive via scented blossom, fat pods, flamboyant blooms and sweet fruit, then drop into the soft earth. Throughout winter, they wait silently before the warmth of the new season awakens them. After the spring equinox, or Ostara, shoots and leaves gradually emerge, unfurling and stretching towards the sun. Seeds promise new life when everything is tired and old. They defy despair.

Sowing seeds during spring is an important moment in the turning year; both a practical and a symbolic activity. It is a wonderful anticipatory task: as you sow, you imagine the plant that will flourish later in the year, bursting into bloom, bushy with aromatic leaves or heavy with edible crops. You are helping to generate life and, in the process, fill your herb cabinet. Spring is also a time to take stock of your own life and plant metaphorical seeds, by planning a way to realize a long-held dream, perhaps, or set an intention.

The transformation of a dry, seemingly unremarkable seed into a lush, beautiful flower or, even more spectacularly, a new tree, is a wonderful thing. The process is so incredible that it can feel like only magic can explain it. Of course, botanical science does have an explanation, but that does not belittle the wonder of the mighty seed. The power of a tiny seed is unimaginable.

HOW SEEDS WORK

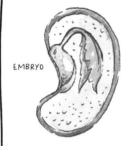

SEED COAT

EMBRYO

FOOD STORE

Every seed, whether it's tiny or huge and woody, like a coconut, contains the embryo plant and a store of food. It also has an outer skin with a minute pore that allows water in and a small scar where it was originally attached to the mother plant.

Most plants produce huge numbers of seeds and have different methods of dispersal to guarantee reproductive success. Some rely solely on the wind to scatter them, while others have wings or cunning hooks to catch in an animal's fur to carry them further. The shape of each seed is designed so that when it falls to the ground it lies in the best position for germination.

SEEDS IN FOLKLORE

Seed sowing has always been accompanied by various rituals in farming communities. In parts of the UK, people would dance with their arms in the air, to alert the gods to provide the rain and strong, healthy crops. In Devon, it was thought to be bad luck to sow seeds during the first three days of March, which were therefore known as 'blind days'. Many communities blessed the seeds before sowing. A Scottish charm, 'The Consecration of the Seed', is one such blessing:

I will go out to sow the seed
In the name of Him who gave it growth;
I will place my front in the wind,
And throw a gracious handful on high.
Should a grain fall on a bare rock,
It shall have no soil in which to grow;
As much as falls to earth,
The dew will make it to be full.

In India, black mustard seeds are scattered across thresholds to protect homes from evil spirits. During the Hindu festival of Pitru Paksha, offerings of black sesame seeds and water are made while chanting mantras to attract dead relatives to earth, relieving them from the cycle of birth and death.

MAGIC SEEDS

Some seeds can be used for magical purposes in their own right. Their latent power and potency can be harnessed and used in charms and spells, especially around love and fertility. Larger seeds, such as mustard, can be incorporated into a mixture for a love sachet, for example, or ground and used for incense. Then, the smoke can be used for divinatory purposes and to communicate with the dead.

Cultivate your dreams

The growth cycle of a seed can serve as a powerful way to cultivate an idea or to manifest a desire.

First, choose seeds of a plant that you feel a connection with – the examples in this book will help you to find the right one. Hold them in your hands and, as you take a deep breath in, visualize new life springing from the soil. As you breathe out, picture the sun entering the seed and triggering it into growth. Do that twice more. Place your cupped hands gently on the compost and send the seeds your love and energy. Thank them for the new life they will bring.

Now sow your seeds. As you do so, think about your idea or desire and imagine it coming into your life. Write it on a piece of paper and tuck it under the seed tray.

You might also like to bless the seed. This is a lovely blessing:

By the power of the water and the power of the earth, by the power of the season's sacred dance, let abundance be given birth. And all good things my life enhance.
(Thanks, lleweylln.com)

When the seeds have germinated, prick them out and pot them on (see page 11 for instructions) so that you have one or two good, strong seedlings. Bury your piece of paper beside them, taking care not to disturb their roots. Water and, later, feed your plants and, as they grow and flourish, so will what you desire until, eventually, it too becomes a beautiful, life-enriching reality.

Harnessing the magic

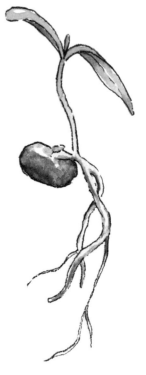

SOWING SEEDS IS ONE OF THE MOST SATISFYING THINGS YOU CAN DO. FROM UNPROMISING BEGINNINGS, A HANDFUL OF TINY BROWN SPECKS IN A POT OF COMPOST WILL GROW INTO A BEAUTIFUL FLOWERING PLANT, A TASTY VEGETABLE CROP OR AN AROMATIC HERB. IT IS A JOYFUL PROCESS THAT MARKS THE END OF WINTER AND THE START OF SPRING. BY SOWING SEEDS, YOU WORK WITH THE TURNING OF THE YEAR BY PLANNING FOR THE SEASONS TO COME. YOU TUNE IN TO NATURE'S CYCLES AND RHYTHMS.

Some seeds germinate quickly, pushing through the compost to unfurl in the light, while others lie dormant for ages – you wonder if they will ever surface, then they too emerge.

One of the many amazing things about seeds is, inside each tiny speck, there is all that is necessary to grow a plant: the embryo and a store of food. Seeds need just three things to get going: water, air and warmth. Once you have provided the correct amounts of all those things, there will be no stopping them – or you.

There is something steadying and meditative about the process of sowing seeds, especially if you allow yourself time to do it mindfully. By following a few simple steps, you can soon have some magical plants, aromatic herbs and all the ingredients needed for a herb cabinet.

HOW TO START

You **could** fling your seeds haphazardly on to a pot of compost or into a flower bed and hope for the best, but this method is more likely to reap rewards.

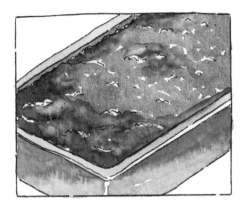

1. Fill a seed tray with seed or multipurpose compost and firm gently with your hands or a tamper (see page 15), so that the compost sits just below the rim.

2. Draw the edge of a flat stick across the top of the tray with a zig-zag movement. This removes surplus compost and creates a level surface.

3. For fine seeds, mix a very small handful with a similar amount of fine sand. Then you can see where you are scattering them and do so evenly. Simply scatter medium-sized seeds and plant larger seeds individually into pots or modules.

4. Sprinkle fine or medium-sized seeds round the edges of the tray first, then fill in the middle. It's better to sow too thinly than too thickly, so the seedlings' roots don't get tangled up.

5. Sieve a light covering of compost over fine seeds to keep them in place, like icing sugar on a cake. Alternatively, use vermiculite, which is a natural material available at garden centres.

6. Stand the seed tray in a tray of water so the compost will draw up moisture from below – watering would disturb the seeds. Remove once moisture has seeped through to the top.

7. Put in a warm, light place to germinate, either in a heated propagator, or on a sunny windowsill covered with a plastic bag to retain humidity, is ideal.

8. Label each batch of seeds with the name of the variety and the date you sowed them.

9. Remove the lid or the bag as soon as seedlings appear, to increase ventilation: new plants need air to thrive.

10. Water regularly and gently, ensuring that the compost does not dry out.

THEN IT'S TIME FOR PRICKING OUT

Once the seedlings emerge, you may find they jostle one another for space. This could be because you sowed them a little too thickly or the seeds were so small it was impossible to tell where they fell. Carefully remove and discard the weakest ones. Work carefully with your fingers or tweezers to pull out ones in the most congested areas. This will give the remainder enough space to keep growing well.

If you have sown seeds in a module, simply move each seedling into a 9cm (3½in) pot once their roots have filled out.

AND AFTER THAT COMES POTTING ON

Once the seeds have sprouted true leaves – that is, not the first smaller ones but the second – they are large enough to handle and you can pot them on. Fill some 9cm (3½in) pots with multipurpose compost and make a little hole in the centre of each one using a dibber or a pencil. Lift each seedling out of the tray, then, with your finger and thumb, hold the leaves, taking care not to damage the stem, and carefully lower it into the hole. Firm the compost around it, water gently and put somewhere warm until the last frosts have passed. Keep the seed packets to refer to transplanting and other details.

FINALLY ... PLANTING OUT

When your seedlings have grown into small plants and their roots have filled the pots, put them outside for a week or two before you plant them out. This is called 'hardening off' and will help the plants get used to outdoor conditions.

Before planting, give the seedlings a good water, then find the best positions for them, referring to the information on the seed packets you saved. Some like it shady, while others prefer full sun. Weed the area, then dig a hole about the same size as the pot. Pop the plant out of the pot and into the hole, making sure the surface of the compost is level with the surface of the soil. Fill any gaps with more soil, firm in gently, then water generously.

SOWING DIRECTLY INTO THE GROUND

Some seeds, such as annuals and certain vegetables, do perfectly well if sown straight into the soil. Make sure the danger of frosts has passed, choose an appropriate position for the species and size of your chosen seeds (check the information given on the seed packets), then prepare the soil and sow. Remember to water them in with a watering can fitted with a fine rose, so you don't dislodge the seeds, and label each row, so you don't mistake the seedlings for weeds and dig them up.

Spring

Summer

MOST TENDER
AND HALF-HARDY
FLOWERS. PLANT OUT
IN LATE SPRING OR
EARLY SUMMER

BIENNIAL FLOWERS,
SUCH AS FOXGLOVES
AND HOLLYHOCKS,
AND FAST-GROWING
HERBS

WHEN TO SOW WHAT

TENDER AND HALF-
HARDY FLOWERS
THAT NEED A LONG
GROWING SEASON

WINTER
VEGETABLES

Late Winter

Autumn

What you need

PART OF THE MAGIC OF GROWING PLANTS FROM SEED IS THAT IT COSTS VERY LITTLE AND ONE PACKET CAN PRODUCE LOTS OF PLANTS. THEN, IF YOU COLLECT SEEDS FROM THE PLANTS YOU GROW (SEE PAGE 24 FOR HOW), YOU WILL HAVE NEW PLANTS FOR FREE.

There are a few basic things that you will need to germinate your seeds and grow strong, healthy seedlings.

FIND YOUR SEEDS ...

During the winter months, much pleasure can be had from leafing through seed catalogues or digging about on seed websites to decide what to grow. Also, use the list of plants in this book as your guide: they all have magical properties and can be grown from seed. In time, you will start collecting your own seeds in the autumn and storing them to sow in the spring.

GET A CONTAINER ...

Wide, flat seed trays, which you can buy from garden centres and elsewhere, are best for sowing fine and medium-sized seeds. Larger seeds can be sown individually in 9cm (3½in) pots or any other container that has good drainage. Yoghurt pots and plastic food trays, for example, work perfectly well, providing you make holes in the bottom so that excess water can drain away. If you don't do this, the seeds will rot.

The cardboard tubes inside toilet rolls or ones made from paper are good for larger seeds too. Sit them upright on a tray next to one another and fill with compost.

Another good option for larger seeds is modules. Sow two seeds per cell, so you have a reserve. Later, the weaker seedling in each cell can be discarded and, once the stronger ones have established a good root structure, they can be either potted on or planted directly outside.

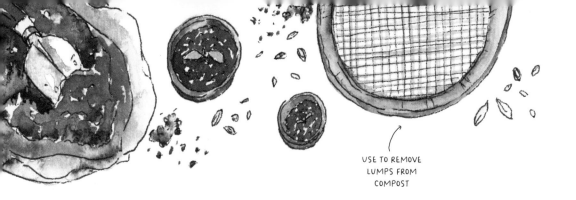

USE TO REMOVE
LUMPS FROM
COMPOST

NOW YOU NEED COMPOST ...

As seeds contain everything they require to
grow, you don't need a special seed compost
for them to germinate – peat-free multipurpose
compost is fine. Don't be tempted to use soil
from the garden, however: it is too heavy. A bag
of vermiculite – a natural growing medium that
is light and keeps the moisture in the compost
– is useful for covering the seeds after sowing.

YOU MIGHT NEED A SIEVE ...

You can buy garden sieves to remove lumpy
bits from compost, but a wire kitchen sieve
or even a tea strainer will do this job just as
well. Doing this is a good idea as lumps may
obstruct the growth of the seedlings' roots.

THEN YOU NEED SOMETHING TO FIRM
THE COMPOST ...

It is worth making a simple device to tamp
down the seeds and the compost. Take a
piece of thin wood 14 x 20cm (5½ x 8in)
and, using wood glue, stick a baton
to the centre (see illustration).
Use it to ensure that the seeds
make good contact with the
compost by firming it a little.

TAMPER

A HEATED PROPAGATOR IS
THE DREAM ...

Put the seed tray into a
propagator (or place on a heated mat or
tray made for this purpose) to give the
seeds a kick start. There is nothing like the
regulated warmth and shelter these provide
to get the germination process going.

... BUT A PLASTIC BAG WILL DO

If you don't have a propagator, put your
seed tray inside a plastic bag until you see
the seedlings sprout. This will create the
warm, humid conditions they relish.

A WATERING CAN IS ESSENTIAL ...

Get the seeds going by placing the seed trays in a bowl or tray of water (see page 10). Then, you will need to water them regularly so the compost doesn't dry out. Use a watering can with a fine rose (the head on the spout). A heavy stream of water will dislodge the seeds and seedlings. A plant sprayer or mister can be a better option, as gentleness is key in the early stages.

LABEL YOUR SEEDS WHEN SOWING

... AS ARE PLANT LABELS

You may think that you will remember what seeds you sowed where, but chances are you won't if you don't keep a record. Buy a bunch of labels and write the information on with a pencil or erasable pen: that way you can reuse the labels. Wooden ones are best ecologically, but usually don't last more than one growing season. Alternatively, make your own labels from stiff cardboard, although you will only be able to use those once too.

SOMETIMES A DIBBER IS A GOOD IDEA

When you come to prick out and pot on, you need to extract each seedling carefully and insert it into a hole you have made in readiness. A small dibber can help with this, but you could also use a pencil or a plant label.

HAVE SMALL PLANT POTS AT THE READY

These are to transfer your seedlings into, so they can grow into healthy plants.

DIBBER

READ THIS BEFORE SOWING

This book will give you the knowledge to grow 100 different plants*, most of them from seeds, but be careful, not all seeds are the same. Some can simply be sprinkled on bare earth and left to do their thing, but others require more attention. The ones rated hard (see Difficulty Rating) often need a period of 'stratification'. This is the process of simulating natural conditions to trigger germination. Some seeds need cold to do the trick, so keeping them in the fridge over winter simulates this. Other seeds need a warm and moist environment instead. The symbols will alert you to how easy or difficult each plant is to sow and grow.

*Apart from very poisonous plants, which are included for reference only.

🌱	EASY
🌱	MEDIUM
🌿	HARD

DIFFICULTY RATING
A single leaf symbol indicates a simple sowing process – usually in a seed tray or directly where the plant is to flower. Two leaves means that a plant requires more attention – a light covering of compost, for example. Three leaves means the seeds will probably need to have some special treatment.

🧺	WHEN TO COLLECT SEEDS
📦	WHEN AND HOW TO SOW SEEDS
🌷	FLOWERING TIME
↕🌱	HEIGHT

SEED INFORMATION
Each plant has a set of symbols to guide you through the process of growing the seed. The basket indicates the best time to harvest seeds, the seed packet when and the best way to sow them, the flower when the plant blooms, and the plant with arrows reveals its eventual height.

TOXICITY
A few of the plants included are poisonous. Be especially wary of the ones with the red symbol, which should be handled with care, wearing gloves, and never be ingested. Information is given as to which parts are toxic – in one or two cases, it is the entire plant.

⬤	MILDLY TOXIC
⬤	TOXIC
⬤	POISONOUS

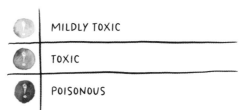

1 ⚑ GARLIC

P *(ALLIUM SATIVUM)*
★ *also known as stinkweed*

packed with vitamins

Few kitchens anywhere in the world are without garlic. Originally from India and Central Asia, it has long been cultivated as a seasoning and a medicinal herb. Its seeds are enclosed in a papery sheath in the flowers, but rarely ripen. To grow garlic, use cloves split from bulbs.

Garlic is packed with vitamins and minerals, plus allicin, a compound with antibacterial and anti-inflammatory properties. The Greek physician Hippocrates recommended it for infections, wounds, cancer, even leprosy, and Egyptian builders chewed it to give them strength when building the pyramids.

THE MAGIC OF GARLIC

Perhaps due to its reputation as a cure-all, garlic has a magical status. Most notoriously, it is believed to keep vampires at bay, but almost every country has its own ideas as to this bulb's powers, such as shielding against bad weather, monsters, blows from enemies, deterring unwanted lovers and preventing nightmares. Brides once carried a clove on them for good luck.

WILD GARLIC

Alium ursinum appears in damp woodlands in spring, especially beside streams. The froth of white flowers make it easy to identify. All parts of the plant are edible. With a milder flavour than garlic, it is great in salads, soup, mashed potato, and can be made into pesto. Remember to only take what you need.

🧺 FLOWERS OFTEN DON'T PRODUCE SEEDS, SO USE CLOVES INSTEAD

◆ LATE AUTUMN, AS NEEDS A PERIOD OF COLD, TO HARVEST THE FOLLOWING SUMMER

🌱 IN LATE SUMMER, WHEN THE TOPS HAVE DIED DOWN, LIFT AND LEAVE THE BULBS TO DRY OUT UNDER COVER. THE BEST CAN BE KEPT TO GROW MORE GARLIC THE FOLLOWING YEAR

↕🌱 UP TO 60CM (2FT)

Uses WIDELY IN COOKING TO ADD FLAVOUR AND FOR ITS HEALTH BENEFITS. EATEN RAW OR AS A TEA, IT CAN EASE VARIOUS COMPLAINTS, BUT CHEW PARSLEY AFTERWARDS TO DISGUISE THE SMELL! IT IS ALSO A GOOD PICK-ME-UP TONIC FOR HENS.

2 ⟩ LEMON BALM

loved by bees

℘ *(MELISSA OFFFICINALIS)*
★ *also known as sweet balm, bee balm, melissa*

Anyone and everyone can grow lemon balm. In fact, it's hard to keep it in check. Once you have introduced it to your patch, it will crop up everywhere and need very little attention (bar cutting back after flowering), which is good news for bees, as they love it. Indeed, beekeepers have been known to plant it near their hives to ensure that their bees don't stray. It is also attributed with the power to bring cheer and banish melancholy and has been prescribed for both for centuries.

THE MAGIC OF LEMON BALM
Culpeper, in his *Complete Herbal*, says that it will 'expel those melancolly vapors from the Spirits.' Scatter leaves in the bath to attract love (lemon balm's planetary ruler is Venus) or wear as a charm to bring suitors scampering towards you.

SEEDS

🧺 LATE SUMMER OR EARLY AUTUMN, BUT NO NEED AS SELF-SEEDS WIDELY. CUT BACK HARD AFTER FLOWERING TO STOP IT BECOMING INVASIVE

🌱 EARLY SPRING

🌼 JULY TO AUGUST

↕🌿 30 TO 90CM (12IN TO 2FT 11IN)

Uses: ENJOY LEMON BALM AS A TEA. LET LEAVES INFUSE FOR ABOUT 15 MINUTES TO ALLOW THE FLAVOUR TO DEVELOP, SWEETENING WITH HONEY. IT'S GOOD TO DRINK BEFORE GOING TO BED, AS IT'S SAID TO PROMOTE RESTFUL SLEEP AND CALM THE NERVES. LEMON BALM CAN ALSO ADD A LEMONY ACCENT TO ICE-CREAM AND FLAVOUR FISH DISHES.

3 ❧ SWEET CICELY

🌱 *(MYRRHIS ODORATA)*
★ *also known as sweet fern, wild myrrh, Roman plant*

This tall plant, with its ferny leaves and umbels of white flowers, may look like cow parsley and hogweed (the latter is poisonous, so steer clear of it), but one sniff of its leaves clearly identifies it. All parts of the plant smell (and taste) strongly of sweet anise – a flavour happily harnessed in various culinary dishes, aperitifs and digestifs. All parts have also been used in medicine, principally to aid digestion, by chewing the seeds, and relieve coughs. The seeds can also be pounded into a pulp and used to polish furniture.

naturally sweet

Uses

SWEET CICELY IS A 'SUGAR SAVER' HERB — THAT IS, ITS NATURAL SWEETNESS MEANS, IF IT IS ADDED TO FRUIT DISHES, LESS SUGAR IS NEEDED. ADDING CHOPPED LEAVES TO GOOSEBERRIES, RHUBARB OR REDCURRANTS WILL REDUCE THEIR ACIDITY.

🧺 FROM MID SUMMER, AS THEY RIPEN

🌰 AUTUMN, IN A SEED TRAY, OR DIRECTLY WHERE THEY ARE TO FLOWER (A PERIOD OF COLD IS NEEDED FOR GERMINATION). SEEDS CAN TAKE UP TO 8 MONTHS TO GERMINATE

🌷 MAY, JUNE

 UP TO 1.5M (4FT 11IN)

4 ⊳ CATMINT

♀ *(NEPETA CATARIA)*
★ *also known as cat's delight, catnip, catwort, field balm*

Anyone who has both a cat and a catmint plant will have witnessed the euphoric moment (for the cat) when the two come together. The penetrating minty scent of catmint is irresistible to felines, sending them into supine rapture. (The dried leaves have also been known to be smoked by humans seeking a mildly hallucinogenic effect.)

A perennial herb, catmint is easy to grow from seed. In early summer it is a froth of pale blue flowers, growing in whorls on long stems. It's not just cats who love it, bees and butterflies do, too, especially peacocks and small tortoiseshells.

THE MAGIC OF CATMINT
Combine catmint with rose petals and put into a cloth sachet to attract love. Pick and press its larger leaves to use as bookmarks in magical books. It can also be chewed to boost courage.

SEEDS LIKE A SUNNY SPOT

Uses A TISANE MADE FROM THE FLOWERING TOPS OF CATMINT CAN SOOTHE A TROUBLED STOMACH AND EASE MENSTRUAL DISCOMFORT. IT IS ALSO A GOOD, MILDLY STIMULATING, TONIC.

🧺 SEPTEMBER

🌱 SPRING, DIRECTLY WHERE THEY ARE TO FLOWER, IN A SUNNY SPOT

🌺 JUNE TO AUGUST

🌱 UP TO IM (3FT 3IN)

5 ❯ MINT

P (MENTHA)
★ *species include spearmint, green spine, mackerel mint, spire mint, peppermint*

A generous plant, mint spreads itself around, shooting its roots through the soil to pop up everywhere. There are many different varieties, including spearmint, peppermint, Moroccan and chocolate mint. Keep mint fresh by using it: cutting back encourages new, fresh growth.

Mint is named after Minthe, a water nymph in Greek mythology adored by Hades, King of the Underworld. His wife Persephone and his sister didn't approve, so one of them turned her into a mint plant.

The menthol in mint leaves freshens and cools and is a key ingredient in toothpaste. It also settles the stomach, so crops up in indigestion tablets and digestive treatments. A few leaves applied to the temples can soothe a headache.

THE MAGIC OF MINT
Folklore has it that a sprig of mint in a pail of milk will prevent it from souring. Place a few leaves in your purse to attract money. To have a wish granted, write the wish on a piece of paper, wrap it in spearmint leaves, then wrap that in a red cloth sewn with red thread. Your wish will be granted by the time the scent of the mint fades.

Uses
THE EASIEST AND MOST EFFECTIVE WAY TO HARNESS THE BENEFITS OF MINT IS TO DRINK IT AS A TEA. IT IS COOLING ON A HOT DAY, REFRESHING ON ALL DAYS AND AIDS DIGESTION. IT IS ALSO SAID TO STIMULATE THE BRAIN AND KEEP YOU ALERT WHEN YOU ARE FLAGGING.

 SNIP FLOWERS OFF WHEN THEY HAVE TURNED BROWN, PUT IN A PAPER BAG AND ALLOW TO DRY OUT FOR AROUND 2 WEEKS. WHEN DRY, CRUSH FLOWERS IN YOUR HANDS TO RELEASE THE SEEDS

SPRING, DIRECTLY AFTER THE LAST FROSTS, IN PARTIAL SHADE

SUMMER

30 TO 40CM (12IN TO 1FT 3IN)

6 ⬦ DILL

♀ *(ANETHUM GRAVEOLENS)*
★ *also known as dilly,*
buzzalchippet, dill weed

Tall with feathery leaves and yellow flowers in umbels, dill is an attractive addition to any garden, although it needs plenty of room. Its common name, 'dill', comes from an old Norse word, 'dylla', which means to soothe or lull, and it has a history of use in herbal medicine, especially as a treatment for coughs and headaches. An annual herb, it produces copious numbers of seeds that, once collected, can be kept in a freezer or a lidded jar in a dry place.

KEEP SEEDS
IN A JAR

THE MAGIC OF DILL
Known as the 'magician's herb', historically, dill was used to offer protection from bad magic and malevolent spirits. As an old rhyme had it, 'The vervain and the dill, That hindreth witches of their will'. As it produces great numbers of seeds, it is used in spells to attract wealth. The scent of it is said to cure hiccups.

🧺 SEPTEMBER – CUT THE WHOLE PLANT DOWN AND DRY THE SEEDS INDOORS

🌱 EARLY TO MID SUMMER, SOW DIRECTLY IN A SUNNY SPOT

🌷 JULY TO SEPTEMBER

↨🌱 UP TO 60CM (2FT)

Uses ALL PARTS OF THE PLANT ARE AROMATIC AND CAN BE USED IN COOKING. IT COMPLEMENTS FISH DISHES PERFECTLY. TRY CHOPPING INTO CREAM CHEESE FOR A TASTY SANDWICH FILLING OR ADDING TO SOUP AND SALADS. CHEW DILL SEEDS TO SWEETEN THE BREATH. ALTERNATIVELY, INFUSE A SMALL NUMBER OF RIPE SEEDS IN A CUPFUL OF BOILING WATER, LEAVE FOR A FEW MINUTES, THEN YOU HAVE THE MEANS TO CALM FLATULENCE.

HOW TO HARVEST AND DRY SEEDS

Collect seeds on a dry day – preferably the second of two dry days. Look for seed heads that have turned brown. Dill, fennel, cow parsley and sunflowers are easy to spot and have many seeds. Tap the stems, which should sound hollow, and if seed falls, it is ready. Cut a few stems, tie them together and hang upside down in a paper bag to catch the seeds. Store somewhere dry and dark. When all the seeds have fallen, throw away the seed head. Spread the seeds out on tissue paper on a wire cooling tray and put somewhere warm until they are completely dry: an airing cupboard is perfect.

COLLECTING SEEDS

The best seeds come from the best plants. If you are collecting from your own garden, the process begins, as always, with the soil. Healthy soil will produce healthy plants and good-quality seeds (see page 54 on the joy of compost). As your flowers grow, look out for perfect blooms. Let them go to seed, collect them and they will, in turn, produce more perfect blooms the following year. If you collect seeds from hedgerows and elsewhere, you take more of a chance, but that's nature in all its wild and unruly glory for you.

SMALLER FLOWER SEEDS

These can be tapped out of seed or flower heads, collected in a container as you wander about, such as yoghurt pots, food storage boxes, or paper envelopes. Either dry the seeds on a wire cooling tray or in a very cool oven with the door left ajar. Keep a close eye on the seeds – you don't want to roast them. They will snap when they are fully dry. Put your seeds in little paper envelopes and write the name of the plant and the date you harvested them on the front.

Are you a hedge witch?

If you love to gather herbs, plants and seeds from the woods, fields or hedges, are drawn to herbal remedies and natural magic, are in tune with the changing seasons and prefer to practise alone, you may well be a hedge witch.

This term has been revived in more recent times as many of us turn to the natural world, to folklore and old customs for comfort and inspiration. Some say it derives from wise women who lived on the outskirts of the village being described as beyond the hedge – that is, in the wild – who practised wortcunning, or, herbal remedies. Others say that it means someone who lives in a liminal space, between this and the spirit world. Most commonly, the term 'hedge witch' has come to mean a person who grows, gathers, harvests and dries her own plants for magical or medicinal purposes.

NIGELLA

As you harvest your seeds, take a moment to notice the differences between them. Marigold seeds are curled like tiny ammonites, sweet peas are fat and round, nasturtiums are chunky and ribbed, *Nigella damascena* seeds are like pieces of grit. It is wonderful, almost incredible, to think that they will all emerge from the soil and become beautiful plants.

sweet pea

nasturtium

Only take as many seeds as you really need from the hedgerow. Leave plenty for the birds, insects and to grow into next year's plants.

7 ◀ LEMON VERBENA

🌿 *(ALOYSIA CITRIODORA, SYNONYM: LIPPIA CITRIODORA)*
★ *also known as cidron, herb Louisa*

It is easy to walk past lemon verbena without noticing it – it has an unassuming look about it, with unremarkable leaves and tiny purple or white flowers that rise in spindly spires in late spring. Brush against its leaves, however, and it makes its presence felt – you are immediately hit with a delicious lemony fragrance. The '*citriodora*' part of its Latin name references its citrussy-ness. It can grow up to 1.5m (4ft 11in) high if left to its own devices, so it's best to clip and prune it to keep it bushy and vigorous.

THE MAGIC OF LEMON VERBENA
It can be worn to attract the opposite sex, used in love spells or as an ingredient in incense to dispel negative energy.

🧺 UNFORTUNATELY, LEMON VERBENA SETS FEW VIABLE SEEDS. IT IS BEST TO TAKE CUTTINGS OR BUY PLANTS INSTEAD

🌷 AUGUST, SEPTEMBER

↕️ UP TO 1.5M (4FT 11IN)

Uses LEMON VERBENA IS A SUPREMELY USEFUL HERB WITH MANY CULINARY USES. ADD A LEAF OR TWO TO FRUIT SALADS, HOME-MADE ICE-CREAM AND SUMMER DRINKS FOR A REFRESHING, SHARP FLAVOUR. A TISANE MADE FROM ITS LEAVES MAKES A REFRESHING DRINK. IT IS ALSO A REVIVING ADDITION TO A BATH. SIMPLY POUR BOILING WATER OVER A HANDFUL OF FRESH LEAVES, STEEP UNTIL COLD, STRAIN, THEN ADD TO THE WATER.

8 ⟩ LOVAGE

P (LEVISTICUM OFFICINALE)
★ *also known as love root, sea parsley*

A most rewarding herb to grow from seed, lovage grows vigorously, becoming a tall, handsome plant in very little time, with large leaves that have a celery-like flavour. It dies back in the winter, but will return bigger and better the following year.

THE MAGIC OF LOVAGE
Put a few sprigs in a muslin bag and add to a bath as part of your pre-date getting-ready activities, as it is said it will make you a love-magnet.

SOAK SEEDS
BEFORE SOWING

Uses IN COOKING, ADD LOVAGE WHEN YOU MIGHT CELERY – IN RAGOUTS, SOUPS, STEWS. ITS YOUNG STEMS CAN ALSO BE CANDIED, LIKE ANGELICA, AND USED TO DECORATE CAKES: PLACE IN HOT SYRUP, COOL OVERNIGHT, THEN REPEAT FOUR TIMES BEFORE ROLLING IN GRANULATED SUGAR. THE STEMS CAN ALSO BE USED AS STRAWS FOR A BLOODY MARY.

🧺 SUMMER AND AUTUMN, WHEN THE SEEDS ARE RIPE

🌰 THE SEEDS HAVE A LONG GERMINATION PERIOD. CHOOSE ONLY THE FRESHEST AND SOAK OVERNIGHT BEFORE SOWING IN A POT. TRANSFER TO A LARGER POT AS SEEDLINGS, GROW BEFORE PLANTING OUT

🌼 JULY, AUGUST

↕🌱 UP TO 2M (6FT 6IN)

9 ⚑ WOAD

(ISATIS TINCTORIA)

★ also known as dyer's woad, glastium, ash of Jerusalem

A member of the *Brassicaceae* (mustard) family, woad has dark green leaves and startlingly bright yellow flowers that grow in huge clusters in spring. A native of Turkey, southern France and Mediterranean, it now flourishes all over Europe. In the USA, however, it is classified as a noxious weed and cultivation is not recommended. For this reason, don't let it self-seed (it produces masses of seeds) and keep a few plants, digging up the rest after flowering so it doesn't take over.

natural dye

LARGE
SEED PODS

THE MAGIC OF WOAD
Famously, it was made into blue body war paint by Picts and Iceni to frighten their enemies.

Uses THE LEAVES CAN BE USED TO MAKE AN INDIGO FABRIC DYE. THIS IS A LENGTHY PROCESS, REQUIRING A LOT OF LEAVES, SO PROPER INSTRUCTION SHOULD BE SOUGHT ON HOW TO DO IT.

🧺 AUGUST, WHEN THE SEEDS ARE A DARK PURPLE BROWN BUT HAVE SOME GREEN, CUT DOWN THE ENTIRE STALKS AND DRY FULLY

🌱 MARCH, APRIL, IN SEED TRAYS, OR DIRECTLY WHERE THEY ARE TO FLOWER

🌷 APRIL, MAY

↕🌱 UP TO 1.2M (3FT 11IN)

10 › APPLE

☘ (MALUS)
★ also known as bee balm

Every garden can have an apple tree (there are many dwarf varieties that can be grown in pots). Boughs of gorgeous blossom in spring are followed by the miracle of apples, slowly swelling into fruit to be picked in the autumn.

Apples have long been a symbol of fruitfulness, prosperity and rejuvenation. There is the fateful fruit eaten in the Garden of Eden, Dionysus' apple, given to Aphrodite, and Lazy Laurence and Awd Goggie, spirits, who protect English apple orchards ... the stories and characters are endless.

THE MAGIC OF APPLES
Cut an apple in half across its middle. The seeds are arranged in a five-pointed star or pentagram, a potent symbol for witchcraft and many different faiths.

BLOSSOM

Once a year, usually on Twelfth Night, people gather in English apple orchards. They are there to wassail: to awaken the spirit of the trees from slumber, to drink their health from a wassailing bowl filled with cider, and to honour the oldest tree in the orchard. Cider-soaked toast is placed in the tree (known as the Apple Tree Man) for the robins, which embody the spirit of the tree. Cider is also poured at its roots, to encourage benevolent spirits and a good crop, while shots are fired through the branches to scare the evil ones away.

Johnny Appleseed (real name John Chapman, 1774–1847) roamed the Far West of the USA, planting apple pips he had collected from cider mills. The result of his life's work was providing the states of Ohio, Illinois, Indiana with a goodly supply of apples.

Uses TO GET RID OF A WART, RUB IT WITH THE CUT HALVES OF AN APPLE, THEN BURY BOTH PIECES. AS THE APPLE DECAYS, THE WART WILL VANISH. TO TELL THE FUTURE, TWIST AN APPLE STALK WHILE RECITING THE ALPHABET. THE LETTER SPOKEN WHEN THE STALK BREAKS IS YOUR FUTURE PARTNER'S INITIAL.

🧺 AUTUMN

◆ APPLE SEEDS NEED TO BE EXPOSED TO COLD FOR SEVERAL WEEKS. PUT IN A BAG OF DAMP MOSS IN A FRIDGE FOR ABOUT

6 WEEKS. BEWARE — EVEN THEN THERE IS ONLY A 30 PER CENT GERMINATION RATE

🌷 MAY

🌱 DEPENDS ON VARIETY

11 PURSLANE

P *(PORTULACA OLERACEA)*
★ *also known as pigweed, pursley, little hogweed*

The pretty yellow flowers and succulent leaves of purslane are grown all over the world. Often disregarded as a weed as it grows so easily and prolifically, its fleshy leaves are good to eat and have, historically, been drunk as a tonic. Purslane makes an attractive addition to a herb garden.

THE MAGIC OF PURSLANE

It was said that if you laid leaves of purslane on your bed, you would not have nightmares. If carried, it was supposed to draw good luck (soldiers took it with them to battle), attract love and, when sprinkled around the home, bring happiness.

SEEDS CAN BE EATEN RAW

Uses THE LEAVES HAVE A TANGY, APPLEY FLAVOUR AND CAN BE EATEN IN SALADS, STIR-FRIED OR COOKED LIKE SPINACH AND SERVED WITH A KNOB OF BUTTER. THE SEEDS CAN ALSO BE EATEN, RAW OR POUNDED INTO A FLOUR.

🧺 EARLY SUMMER, BEFORE THE SEEDS SCATTER. ONE CONE-SHAPED CAPSULE CONTAINS MANY TINY, OVAL-SHAPED SEEDS

THE SEEDS WITH SOIL, AS THEY NEED LIGHT TO GERMINATE. LEAVES WILL BE READY TO PICK IN 6 TO 8 WEEKS

🌱 SPRING TO LATE SUMMER, DIRECTLY WHERE THEY ARE TO FLOWER, IN A SUNNY SPOT. DO NOT COVER

🌷 JULY, AUGUST

🌱 UP TO 20CM (8IN)

12 ⟨ PENNYROYAL

𝑃 *(MENTHA PULEGIUM)*
★ *also known as lurk-in-the-ditch, pudding grass*

This member of the mint family creeps along the ground, creating new plants as stems touch the earth and take root. It is easily overlooked until it blooms in summer, its lovely pale-blue flowers growing in pom-poms along the tall spikes. Its leaves have a fresh peppermint scent when crushed and were once used to make a popular drink. Sailors would take pots of pennyroyal on long sea voyages to purify casks of drinking water and to prevent sea sickness.

THE MAGIC OF PENNYROYAL

Putting a few leaves in your shoe is said to prevent weariness when travelling. Considered a herb of peace, it was given to quarrelling couples to stop them fighting.

COLLECT SEEDS
IN AUTUMN

peppermint scent

Uses ADD A FEW CHOPPED LEAVES TO SOUPS TO GIVE THEM A GENTLE MINTY FLAVOUR. AN INFUSION OF THE LEAVES IS BELIEVED TO BE GOOD FOR THE DIGESTION. BRING A POT OF PENNYROYAL INDOORS TO KEEP MOSQUITOES OUT.

🧺 SEPTEMBER, OCTOBER   ❀ JULY TO SEPTEMBER

◈ SPRING, DIRECTLY   ↡ FLOWER SPIKES REACH
   WHERE THEY ARE TO   30CM (12IN)
   FLOWER, ONCE DANGER
   OF FROSTS HAS PASSED

13 ◄ FENUGREEK

P (TRIGONELLA FOENUM-GRAECUM)
★ *also known as Greek hay, Greek clover*

It's the seeds that take centre stage with this annual herb. Rich in protein, they are said to have all manner of benefits, including serving as a tonic for convalescents and to stimulate digestion. They are also, of course, a key ingredient in many curry powders and spice mixes. The leafy plant itself, which looks like turbo-charged clover and has white flowers, is less well known but, once established, will provide a steady stream of cut-and-come-again spinach-like greens.

rich in protein

THE MAGIC OF FENUGREEK
There is an old tradition said to bring money to the house: people would half fill a small jar with fenugreek seeds, add a few seeds every day until the jar was full, then empty the jar, composting the contents. Then start again.

Uses
SPROUT FENUGREEK SEEDS FOR A NUTRITIOUS ADDITION TO SALADS OR TO GIVE ADDED CRUNCH IN SANDWICHES. YOU CAN ALSO SOAK THE SEEDS, STRAIN, THEN INFUSE THEM IN BOILING WATER FOR A SOOTHING DRINK. IF A LITTLE BITTER, ADD HONEY OR BROWN SUGAR. SAUTÉ LEAVES WITH GARLIC AND LEMON AS A SIDE DISH.

🧺 EITHER BUY FROM A SUPERMARKET OR HARVEST YOUR OWN IN AUTUMN. THE SEEDS ARE IN YELLOW PODS AND READY TO GATHER 30 TO 35 DAYS AFTER FLOWERING

◆ LATE SPRING, DIRECTLY WHERE THEY ARE TO FLOWER, IN A SUNNY SPOT

🌱 EARLY TO MID SUMMER

↕🌱 UP TO 30CM (12IN)

14 ◄ FENNEL

P *(FOENICULUM VULGARE)*
★ *also known as sweet fennel, samar, sheeh*

Standing tall with feathery leaves, this elegant biennial or short-lived perennial looks as good in a flower bed as it does in a herb garden or vegetable patch. All parts of it are aromatic and edible and have a variety of uses, medicinal, culinary and magical. It is easy to grow from seed – the seeds themselves are valued in cooking and in herbal remedies, especially for eyesight – and once it gets going, there's no stopping it. There is a Welsh saying: 'He who seeds fennel and gathers it not is not a man but a devil.' So let that be a warning not to forget to harvest its deliciously aniseedy leaves and stalks.

THE MAGIC OF FENNEL

Bunches of fennel can be hung over doors on Midsummer Eve to keep fire from your home and ensure freedom from enchantment. Those who kept horses used it to persuade difficult animals to harness. Another rather niche custom is to wear a piece of fennel in your left shoe to prevent wood ticks biting your legs. It is also used in purification sachets and healing mixtures.

Uses ADD SOME SEEDS OR FRONDS IF POACHING WHITE FISH OR TO A SAUCE. FLAVOUR BREAD, SAVOURY BISCUITS OR SOUP WITH GROUND OR WHOLE SEEDS. AN INFUSION OF SEEDS CAN SOOTHE TIRED EYES. IN INDIA, CHEWING SEEDS IS SAID TO HELP EYESIGHT.

🧺 LATE SUMMER – CUT WHOLE SEED HEADS, DRY, THEN COLLECT SEEDS

🌷 JULY TO NOVEMBER

↕🌱 UP TO 1.5M (4FT 11IN)

🔶 MID SPRING, DIRECTLY WHERE THEY ARE TO FLOWER, IN MOIST, WELL-DRAINED SOIL, IN A SUNNY SPOT

15 ▷ CARAWAY

P (CARUM CARVI)
★ also known as alcaravea, kummel

The seeds are the most important part of
caraway plants, and are used in baking and
to make kummel liqueur. It is easy to grow
plants of your own, so long as you sow
the seeds in a sunny place as, in the wild,
caraway favours sun-baked mountainsides.
They will also be happy in a sunny window
box or container. Seeds germinate quickly and
the plant will reach 20cm(8in) in the first year
and its full height in the second. You will be
rewarded with a light and airy plant with white
flowers and feathery leaves. Harvest the seeds
when they are fully ripe but before the oblong
case that contains them bursts open. The roots
can also be dug up and cooked like carrots.

loves the sun

THE MAGIC OF CARAWAY
A caraway-seed biscuit is said to induce lust.
Chewing the seeds is supposed to improve
the memory. In the Middle Ages,
women sewed caraway
seeds into the clothing
of men as they went
on crusades, to keep
them faithful.

Uses TO MAKE CARAWAY TEA,
INFUSE ONE TSP CRUSHED SEEDS IN A
POT OF BOILING WATER. IT CAN CALM A
WINDY DIGESTIVE SYSTEM. SPRINKLE
SEEDS ON CABBAGE TO MAKE IT EASIER
TO DIGEST.

 WHEN THE PLANT HAS TURNED
YELLOW AND THE SEEDS ARE A
STRAW COLOUR

JUNE TO JULY

UP TO 60CM (2FT)

 LATE SUMMER OR EARLY AUTUMN,
WHERE THEY ARE TO FLOWER

16 ◢ PUMPKIN

(CUCURBITA MAXIMA)
★ also known as jack-o'-lantern

easy to grow

The pleasingly round, orange fruits are a wonderful sight in autumn, either growing or as part of Halloween celebrations. Native to North America and Mexico, the pumpkin is one of the oldest domesticated plants, providing nourishing meals for centuries. Inside its ribbed skin is the edible pulp and a multitude of large seeds, to either collect and eat or sow to grow more.

DELICIOUS SEEDS

THE MAGIC OF PUMPKINS

Synonymous with Halloween (or Samhain), hollowed out, carved and lit from within, jack-o'-lanterns, as they are called, sit on many doorsteps and windowsills on 31 October. This tradition started in Ireland and Scotland when turnips and mangel-wurzels (a large type of beet) were left burning on farm gateposts and in stables to deter harmful spirits and the souls of the dead, who wandered about at this time. In the West of England, this was known as 'Punkie Night' ('punkie' is an Old English word for 'lantern'). Children marched around with a jack-o'-lantern, chanting songs and threatening anyone who didn't give them treats – a precursor to trick or treating.

Uses TOAST SEEDS FOR A SNACK AND TO ADD TO EVERYTHING! RINSE OFF THE PULP. DRY ON PAPER TOWEL, SEPARATING SO THEY DON'T STICK TOGETHER. SPRINKLE ON TO A BAKING TRAY, TOSS WITH OLIVE OIL AND ROAST IN THE OVEN (180°C/350°F, GAS MARK 4) FOR 5 TO 10 MINUTES. FOR EXTRA PEP, ADD TWO TSP GROUND CUMIN, ONE TSP SMOKED PAPRIKA AND A PINCH OF SEA SALT TO THE OIL.

🧺 SEPTEMBER TO OCTOBER, WHEN FRUITS HARVESTED. WASH SEEDS AND PLACE, NOT TOUCHING, ON PAPER TOWEL UNTIL DRY. STORE IN AN ENVELOPE IN A COOL, DRY PLACE

🌰 APRIL TO MAY, IN SEED TRAYS, PLANTING OUT WHEN SEEDLINGS HAVE A FEW TRUE LEAVES. ALLOW SPACE AND KEEP WELL WATERED AS THEY ARE THIRSTY PLANTS

↕ VERY VARIABLE – ALLOW SPACE

MAKE A HERB GARDEN

Anyone can grow herbs. Even if you have no outdoor space, you can have a few pots brimming with leafy goodness on a windowsill. You don't need much horticultural know-how as most grow easily and quickly from seed (I'm looking at you, coriander), which is very rewarding. What they must have, though, is sunlight, especially during the growing season, as many originate from hot countries so do best if they can bask in the sun. They also need protection in the early days, which is why they are often tucked behind low-growing hedges.

If you have some outdoor space, why not try and grow some herbs of your own?

Which herbs to grow?

For the kitchen:
chervil, chives,
coriander, dill,
marjoram, parsley,
rosemary, sage, tarragon.

To make cosmetics:
chamomile, eyebright,
lady's mantle, marigold,
rosemary, sage, salad
burnet, southernwood,
yarrow.

For herbal remedies:
comfrey, fennel, garlic,
lemon balm, marigold,
marsh mallow, parsley,
peppermint, rosemary,
sage, thyme, vervain.

HERB-GROWING TIP
Herbs have many different uses. See the suggestions above to help you choose which to grow.

It is good to add some organic matter (compost) to the soil and dig out any weeds. Check the seed packets for how big your herbs will grow to and allow reasonable space. Note that mint is very invasive. It can be contained by growing in pots, or by cutting back in autumn.

IF YOU ARE SHORT OF SPACE ...

... FILL A HANGING BASKET
Line the hanging basket first with moss, then a plastic bag, punctured with holes for drainage. This prevents the soil from falling out and keeps moisture in. Use good-quality compost, then pack up to three or four herbs in. Marjoram, sage or thyme are useful and will trail once established. You could also pop in a few nasturtium seeds, for their colourful flowers and pretty leaves, both edible.

... GROW IN A WINDOW BOX
Ideally, position outside the kitchen where it will get light for 4 or 5 hours a day. Most window boxes will take three or four pots, which may be replaced if they flag. Water regularly and feed once all the nutrients in the compost have been used up.

Again, culinary herbs – chives, thyme, sage, parsley or marjoram – and different varieties of mint in pots work well. Add interest with, for example, sage 'Tricolor', which has pink-and-white patterned leaves, golden balm and silver thyme, plus marigolds for a splash of colour.

... PLANT HERBS IN A FLOWER BED
Many herbs look lovely next to flowering plants and shrubs. Angelica, lovage and fennel are statuesque with interesting leaves and flower heads so work well at the back of the border, while lady's mantle (*Alchemilla mollis*) and marjoram are low-growing, perfect for the front.

... REMOVE A PAVING SLAB
If you have a paved patio or terrace, you can lift up a slab or two to create a planting pocket. Simply dig in some compost to improve the soil first, then plant with low-growing evergreen herbs.

seed pods

17 ◀ BLACK MUSTARD

℗ (BRASSICA NIGRA)

mustard flowers

Black mustard is an annual herb that produces edible leaves and bright yellow flowers, followed by pods that contain around 20 globular black seeds. The plant is native to India, but has been cultivated widely throughout the world, due to its extreme usefulness, medically and as a condiment.

In folk medicine, its heat-releasing properties are said to improve the blood supply to the skin, lungs and kidneys. Plasters made from powdered mustard seeds mixed with water are used as a poultice to ease rheumatic and arthritic pain, muscular spasms and strained muscles.

In cooking, the seeds are often 'popped' at the start of curry-making, and the leaves can be eaten like spinach. It is as a condiment, however, that mustard is used most.

TASTY SEEDS

Uses GROW AS A MICROGREEN TO PEP UP SALADS. SOAK A HANDFUL OF SEEDS, FILL A TRAY WITHOUT HOLES WITH COMPOST, SPRINKLE THE SEEDS OVER AND COVER TO BLOCK OUT THE LIGHT. LEAVE FOR TWO TO THREE DAYS, MISTING DAILY. SNIP AND EAT WHEN THE SEEDLINGS ARE 2CM (³/₄IN) OR SO. TO MAKE YOUR OWN MUSTARD, SOAK 100 (3¹/₂OZ) OF MUSTARD SEEDS IN 300ML (1¹/₄IN) OF WHITE WINE VINEGAR OVERNIGHT. STRAIN AND KEEP THE LIQUID. GRIND THE SEEDS TO A PASTE IN A FOOD PROCESSOR. DILUTE WITH THE SAVED LIQUID UNTIL SMOOTH AND TO YOUR LIKING.

THE MAGIC OF MUSTARD

In German folklore, mustard seeds were sown into the hem of a wedding gown to ensure that the bride would achieve dominance in her new home. In India consuming mustard seeds was thought to bestow the power of flight. Italians have been known to sprinkle mustard seeds on to doorsteps to protect the house.

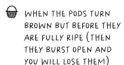 WHEN THE PODS TURN BROWN BUT BEFORE THEY ARE FULLY RIPE (THEN THEY BURST OPEN AND YOU WILL LOSE THEM)

SPRING, DIRECTLY WHERE THEY ARE TO

FLOWER, IN WELL-DRAINED SOIL, IN A SUNNY SPOT

 MAY ONWARDS

 90CM (2FT 11IN)

18 ◁ VERVAIN

🌱 *(VERBENA OFFICINALIS)*
★ *also known as herb of grace*

Another herb that featured in England's witch trials (if you grew it, you were declared a witch), vervain has occupied a central place in folklore for centuries. That is surprising as it is an undistinguished, gangly plant with tiny lilac flowers on coarse spikes (***Verbena officinalis*** var. ***grandiflora*** is a more attractive and elegant variety to try). So venerated was it, that, according to Pliny, it should only be cut by a silver or gold blade, held in the left hand at the rising of Sirius, the Dog Star. The early Christian Church also valued it. Calling it the 'herb of grace', they used it to deal with a variety of unpleasant problems, from gout and piles to driving away snakes and demons , and for sharpening knives.

COLLECT SEEDS IN
SEPTEMBER

THE MAGIC OF VERVAIN

The Romans considered vervain so important that they held a festival to celebrate it, Verbenalia, and used it for divination. According to European folk magic, smearing your naked body with its juice gave you special powers. It was also a common ingredient in love spells.

Uses HERBALISTS AND HOMEOPATHS OFTEN PRESCRIBE VERVAIN TO LIFT DEPRESSION AND AID SLEEP. IT CAN BE DANGEROUS FOR AMATEURS TO USE, SO IT'S BEST TO CONSULT THE EXPERTS.

🧺 SEPTEMBER

◆ LATE SUMMER, DIRECTLY WHERE THEY ARE TO FLOWER, OR SPRING, BUT PREPARE SEEDS 10 DAYS BEFORE, AS NEED COLD TO GERMINATE. SOAK FOR 12 TO 24 HOURS, THEN STORE IN THE FRIDGE IN

A CONTAINER OR PLASTIC BAG IN A SAND AND PEAT MIX FOR 14 DAYS, KEEPING MOIST, THEN SOW DIRECTLY WHERE THEY ARE TO FLOWER

🌱 JUNE TO SEPTEMBER

↕🌱 UP TO 1M (3FT 3IN)

19 ◀ VALERIAN

🌱 *(VALERIANA OFFICINALIS)*
★ *also known as all-heal, setwell, capon's tail, cat's valerian, vandal root*

Attributed with many magical and health-giving powers, valerian is a key plant to grow in the herb garden. Identified by its tiny white flowers and its pungent smell, especially when the leaves are crushed, it grows wild in damp ditches, road verges and along riverbanks. In folk medicine, it's the root, harvested from two- to three-year-old plants in autumn, that is most valued. Dried, it emits a strong, earthy smell a little like stale milk or old socks. Made into a tea (sweetened with honey to make it more palatable), it can be drunk to ease insomnia and calm the nerves. Too much, however, can cause lethargy, so moderation is key.

root

THE MAGIC OF VALERIAN
Chaucer named valerian one of the herbs that witches put in their potions and it has always had occult associations. Among the magical powers credited to it are influencing important people and attracting romantic attention.

HARVEST SEEDS IN
SUMMER

Uses MAKE A DECOCTION (SEE PAGE 104) OF THE ROOTS TO TAKE AS A TONIC OR TO TREAT NERVOUS HEADACHES. PLANT IT NEAR CATMINT (SEE PAGE 21) TO CREATE A PATCH OF CAT HEAVEN — THEY LOVE IT TOO.

🧺 SUMMER, WHEN FLOWER HEADS ARE DRY, KEEPING THE POWDERY SEEDS IN HEADS

SPRING, PLANT THE WHOLE FLOWER HEADS JUST UNDER

THE SURFACE, DIRECTLY WHERE YOU WANT PLANTS TO FLOWER

🌷 JUNE TO SEPTEMBER

UP TO 1.5M (4FT 11IN)

20 THYME

℗ (THYMUS VULGARIS)
★ also known as shepherd's thyme, mother thyme

Thyme is one of the most useful herbs in the kitchen, lending its green, woody savouriness to any number of dishes, and is a key ingredient in herb bundles added to stews and roasts. (It also works well in a potpourri, see page 84.) Fortunately, it is really easy to grow, with many varieties to choose from. Its small, dark-green leaves grow densely on short, woody stems and tiny pale mauve flowers appear in whorls at the tops of them in summer. It also grows in the wild, where the plant has a better flavour and is more fragrant. Bees also love it and thyme honey is delicious.

TINY BLACK
SEEDS

THE MAGIC OF THYME

Like many herbs, Thyme is credited with protecting the home from evil and, put in a pocket, saves the traveller from mishaps. It also had a reputation for instilling courage – crusaders reportedly wore it for this reason. A cup of thyme tea combined with a beer was also considered a cure for shyness. The souls of the dead were said to live in thyme flowers, as were fairies and elves.

Uses APART FROM ITS MANY CULINARY USES, THYME HAS ANTISEPTIC PROPERTIES, SO CAN BE USED AS A POULTICE TO TREAT WOUNDS. IT CAN ALSO BE DRUNK IN A TISANE TO SOOTHE INDIGESTION AND CLEAR THE HEAD.

 LATE SUMMER, WHEN THE FLOWERS ARE DRY

🌷 JULY

⬇🌱 UP TO 23CM (9IN)

MARCH OR APRIL, IN SEED TRAYS. GERMINATION CAN TAKE FROM 14 TO 28 DAYS

21 ◂ SUMMER SAVORY

(SATUREJA HORTENSIS)

★ *also known as herbe de St Julien, garden savory*

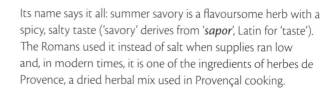

Its name says it all: summer savory is a flavoursome herb with a spicy, salty taste ('savory' derives from '*sapor*', Latin for 'taste'). The Romans used it instead of salt when supplies ran low and, in modern times, it is one of the ingredients of herbes de Provence, a dried herbal mix used in Provençal cooking.

Summer savory is a pretty plant to have in the garden, with small, tubular, mauve flowers that have a pleasant fragrance.

spicy, salty taste

THE MAGIC OF SUMMER SAVORY
Another appetite that is said to be enlivened by savory, is a sexual one. Pliny pointed out that lusty satyrs romped in savory meadows and feasted on it.

Uses USED AS A GARGLE OR DRUNK AS A TISANE, SAVORY LEAVES CAN HELP TO SOOTHE A SORE THROAT.

SOW SEEDS
IN APRIL

🛒 LATE SUMMER, WHEN LEAVES DIE BACK

 EARLY APRIL, DIRECTLY WHERE THEY ARE TO FLOWER

🌱 JULY TO SEPTEMBER

↕🌱 30 TO 60CM (1 TO 2FT)

22 ▶ MOTHERWORT

🌱 *(LEONURUS CARDIACA)*
★ *also known as herb of life, throw-wort, lion's tail*

SEEDS

Motherwort is so called because of the old belief that it eased anxiety during pregnancy and childbirth. It does have a mild sedative quality, so this may be true, although it should be used with caution. The plant is happiest growing where it won't be disturbed, so crops up on waste ground, in ditches and by roadsides. Its white or purple-pink flowers grow from a single tall, square spike and are loved by bees and butterflies. It is a native of Siberia, but has naturalized in Europe and Asia.

THE MAGIC OF MOTHERWORT

Seen as a protective herb, it is used in spells to protect pregnant women and their unborn children. Seventeenth-century English herbalist Nicholas Culpeper thought it 'removed melancholy vapours from the heart'.

🧺 SUMMER, WHEN IN FULL BLOOM, CUT WHOLE PLANT AT BASE AND HANG UPSIDE DOWN TO DRY

🧂 LATE SPRING, BUT PREPARE SEEDS 10 DAYS BEFORE, AS NEED COLD TO GERMINATE. SOAK FOR 12 TO 24 HOURS, THEN STORE

IN THE FRIDGE IN A CONTAINER OR PLASTIC BAG IN A SAND AND PEAT MIX FOR 10 DAYS, KEEPING MOIST. THEN SOW DIRECTLY WHERE THEY ARE TO FLOWER

🌱 EARLY SUMMER

🌱 UP TO IM (3FT 3IN)

Uses IT CAN HAVE A CALMING EFFECT IF DRUNK AS A TEA, SWEETENING WITH HONEY IF IT'S BITTER. MAKE A TINCTURE (SEE PAGE 104) FROM ITS LEAVES AND FLOWERS IMMEDIATELY AFTER YOU HAVE PICKED THEM. USE DILUTED AS A HERBAL REMEDY FOR MENSTRUAL PROBLEMS.

HARVESTING AND PRESERVING HERBS

While it's lovely to pick fresh herbs and use them at once, you can only do that for a limited time. To have some ready all year to use in cooking and in lotions and potions, it is a good idea to dry and store them. The secret is to do it speedily and at a time when the herbs are at their most flavoursome.

HOW TO COLLECT HERBS

Gather leafy herbs when the flowers are in bud but not full open. Do this in the morning, after the dew has dried but before the sun is hot. This is essential if herbs are to maintain their flavour.

Snip the stems with sharp scissors or secateurs. Breaking the stems or pulling at the leaves will damage them.

Wash the herbs quickly and carefully in tepid water. This will remove any dirt or lurking insects.

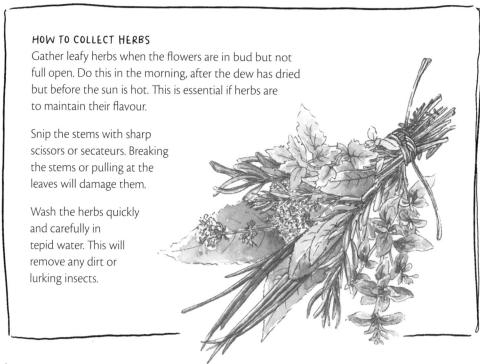

HOW TO DRY THEM

Find a reasonably large tray or a wire cooling rack. Lay the herbs out in a single layer and cover with a thin piece of fabric – muslin is ideal. This is to keep them clean and dust-free. Make sure that there is no extra moisture hiding in the herbs from washing.

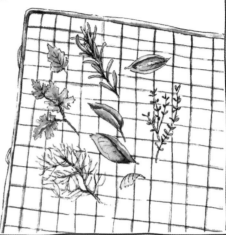

Put the tray or rack in a warm, airy, dark place. An airing cupboard is perfect or the plate-warmer drawer of an oven, set at the lowest temperature, with the door open, or a dark, warm shed. Don't leave in the sun.

Leave for 24 hours or so. The leaves should still be green. If they are brown, they were too hot and the flavour will be lost.

HOW TO STORE THEM

Don't hang about. Herbs need to be stored as soon as they have dried, to avoid coming into contact with any moisture.

Take the leaves off the twigs and rub or crumble them onto a piece of paper.

Pour into small screw-top jars and seal tightly.

Put the jars in a dark cupboard, unless they are made from dark glass. Light causes rapid deterioration in flavour.

Use within nine months. After that, they will lose their flavour, colour and scent.

GOOD HERBS TO DRY

Sage, rosemary, spearmint, lovage, thyme, marjoram. Don't bother with parsley, it loses all its taste.

★ *Because seeds are already dry, they store very well. Coriander seeds are good ones to start with.*

23 ⊳ SOAPWORT

(SAPONARIA OFFICINALIS)
★ *also known as bouncing Bet, tumbling Ted, bruisewort*

This plant's leaves foam when agitated in water, hence its common name. Caused by organic chemicals called saponin, this foaminess benefited American settlers, who used it to make soap and detergent for washing clothes. Culpeper, though, suggested it was a cure for venereal disease.

Soapwort has profuse, pretty, five-petalled flowers that are loved by butterflies – reason enough to grow it.

COLLECT SEEDS
IN SEPTEMBER

leaves foam in water

🧺 SEPTEMBER

📗 LATE WINTER, IN SEED TRAYS, PLANTING OUTDOORS AFTER THE LAST FROSTS, OR IN SPRING, DIRECTLY WHERE THEY ARE

TO FLOWER. GERMINATION TAKES ABOUT 3 WEEKS

🌸 JULY, AUGUST

🌱 UP TO 90CM (2FT 11IN)

Uses HARNESS SOAPWORT'S SOAPINESS BY MAKING A SIMPLE CLEANSER. COVER A HANDFUL OF LEAVES AND STEMS WITH WATER IN A PAN. BRING SLOWLY TO THE BOIL, SIMMER FOR 5 MINUTES, THEN ALLOW TO COOL. STRAIN THE LIQUID THROUGH MUSLIN OR A SIEVE INTO A SCREW-TOP BOTTLE AND STORE IN THE FRIDGE. USE TO CLEANSE ALL TYPES OF SKIN, BUT DON'T HANG ABOUT OR SHARE – IT WILL ONLY KEEP FOR A FEW DAYS.

24 ◖ WORMWOOD

P (ARTEMISIA ABSINTHIUM)
★ *also known as old woman, green ginger, sweet Annie*

bitter

The silvery foliage and yellow flowers of wormwood look unremarkable, but they belie its dangerous reputation. It is the most bitter of all plants and has a history of being used in a wide variety of tricky situations, including 'denying the snake its poyson' (a snake bite antidote, in other words), being burnt with sandalwood to contact the dead, to expel parasitic worms (as practised by the ancient Egyptians) and relieve anus pain of demonic origin! In sixteenth-century England, there were rules about when and how to gather it – when the flowers were still fresh and before it had set seed (although this could be applied to most herbs).

THE MAGIC OF WORMWOOD
It is burnt in incense to develop psychic powers. *Cunningham's Encyclopedia of Magical Herbs* states that it can protect from the bites of sea serpents. It is also, more usefully, one of many herbs used in love potions. A wreath made of wormwood flowers is supposed to bring good luck if thrown on a midsummer fire.

SOW SEEDS
IN SPRING

🧺 SEPTEMBER, CUT DOWN THE WHOLE PLANT, PUT IN A PAPER BAG AND SHAKE OUT THE SEEDS WHEN DRY

🌱 LATE SUMMER

↕🌱 UP TO 60CM (2FT)

◆ SPRING, DIRECTLY WHERE THEY ARE TO FLOWER, AFTER THE LAST FROSTS

Uses WORMWOOD'S MOST POTENT USE IS IN ABSINTHE, AN ADDICTIVE LIQUEUR KNOWN AS THE GREEN WITCH THAT RAN AMOK THROUGH THE ARTISTIC COMMUNITIES OF NINETEENTH-CENTURY FRANCE. DRUNK IN QUANTITY, IT WAS SAID TO PRODUCE MIND-ALTERING EFFECTS (ALTHOUGH THIS HAS SUBSEQUENTLY BEEN DISPROVED), WHICH RESULTED IN A BAN BEING IMPOSED ON IT IN MOST OF EUROPE IN 1915. THIS HAS SINCE BEEN LIFTED. MORE PROSAICALLY, MODERN HERBALISTS USE WORMWOOD AS A TONIC FOR FLATULENCE.

25 PARSLEY

☙ (PETROSELINUM CRISPUM)
★ also known as Devil's oatmeal, persil, rock parsley, herb of death

Parsley's reluctance to germinate (it can take up to six weeks) has given it a reputation as a challenging plant to grow. It was said to go down to the Devil, then back up again after sowing, the wait was so long. The ancient Greeks associated it with death and used it as a funerary herb. It was dedicated to Persephone, wife of Hades and queen of the underworld, and tombs were decorated with parsley wreaths. In British folklore, only 'witches and rogues' were able to grow it successfully, unless you planted it on Good Friday, between noon and 3pm, when the Devil was powerless.

Once it has germinated, parsley is easy to grow and provides much savoury tastiness to no end of dishes, plus lots of vitamin C. Although it is a biennial, it is grown as an annual as the leaves are finer in the first year.

SEEDS

Uses
PARSLEY HAS BEEN USED AS A BREATH FRESHENER SINCE ROMAN TIMES. IT IS ALSO SAID TO STIMULATE DIGESTION AND APPETITE. IT IS FREQUENTLY USED TO FLAVOUR A WHITE SAUCE EATEN WITH FISH AND TO GARNISH SAVOURY DISHES.

THE MAGIC OF PARSLEY
A wreath of parsley worn on the head was said to prevent inebriation, but if you cut parsley when in love, your sweetheart was supposed to die. Transplant parsley and you invite trouble into your life.

🧺 WHEN THE SEED HEADS HAVE TURNED BROWN

🌼 JUNE TO AUGUST, BUT WILL FLOWER THE FOLLOWING YEAR

🌱 FROM EARLY SPRING TO SUMMER, DIRECTLY WHERE THEY ARE TO GROW

↕🌱 UP TO 30CM (12IN)

26 BAY

🌱 *(LAURUS NOBILIS)*
★ *also known as bay laurel, sweet bay, Daphne, heroes' crown*

While there are a number of different laurel trees, bay is the 'true laurel' and the one that we associate with cooking soups and pasta sauces. It was made into a wreath to honour heroes and poets in ancient Greece and Rome, and is the tree that Daphne turned into when chased by Apollo in Greek mythology. An evergreen shrub, hedge or small tree (depending on how you grow it), it is a useful garden plant with many culinary uses.

SEEDS

Uses FRESH BAY LEAVES ADD A SLIGHTLY SPICY FLAVOUR TO SOUPS AND PASTA DISHES. DRIED BAY LEAVES WILL, TOO, BUT THE FLAVOUR WON'T BE AS STRONG. SCATTER A FEW LEAVES INTO A BATH AFTER A LONG WALK OR EXERCISE TO EASE ACHING LIMBS. DRIED BAY LEAVES ARE ALSO AN INSECT REPELLENT.

THE MAGIC OF BAY

Bay was used to stimulate clairvoyance by priestesses in ancient Rome. Today, placing some leaves under your pillow is said to induce prophetic dreams, while putting a few leaves on a windowsill could prevent lightning. Planting a bay tree near home could be a good idea as it is supposed to protect the occupants from illness.

🧺 LATE SPRING. LOOK OUT FOR PURPLISH-BLACK BERRIES, WHICH EACH CONTAIN A SINGLE SEED

◆ SPRING, IN A SEED TRAY. BAY SEEDS TAKE A WHILE TO GERMINATE (UP TO 6

MONTHS); BE PATIENT, KEEP WATCH TO MAKE SURE SEEDS DON'T ROT

🌱 MAY

🌱 UP TO 2M (6FT 6IN)

27 ⟨ BASIL

P *(OCIMUM BASILICUM)*
★ *also known as sweet basil, witches' herb*

This annual herb is one of the easiest to grow from seed indoors. Just remember to keep it somewhere sunny, don't let it dry out and pinch out the tops and flowers to keep it bushy.

Basil's strong and distinctive flavour (which increases when cooked) makes it a useful addition to a windowsill of kitchen herbs. Its flowering stems contain an essential oil and are its medicinal parts. Infusions can sometimes relieve stomach pains and prevent travel sickness.

THE MAGIC OF BASIL

Basil is used in many spells associated with love: one whiff soothes tension between lovers; rubbing leaves against the skin attracts love, as does giving someone a pot of basil as a gift. Witches were said to drink half a cup of basil juice before setting off on their broomsticks.

Uses CAST SOME LEAVES INTO A HOT BATH FOR AN INVIGORATING AND PURIFYING SOAK. CARRY SOME IN YOUR POCKETS TO ATTRACT WEALTH.

seed heads

SEEDS

🧺 ONCE BROWN, SHAKE SEEDS FROM SEED HEADS INTO AN ENVELOPE

🌱 FROM FEBRUARY TO JULY, SOW IN SUCCESSION IN A POT OF COMPOST

🌷 MARCH TO SEPTEMBER

↕🌱 UP TO 60CM (2FT)

28 ⫸ RAGWORT

🌱 ⚪ (SENECIO JACOBAEA)
★ also known as stinking willie, staggerwort, stammerwort, cankerweed

A lover of poor soil, ragwort thrives where other plants do not, by the sides of roads verges, on rubbish tips and waste ground. You will recognize it at once as it is tall, with the yellow petals of its flowers radiating like sunbeams from an orange centre. Frequently dismissed as a weed, it is an important pollinator and loved by butterflies.

It is rarely a problem in gardens, but note that ragwort is a danger to livestock (it contains toxins that can cause liver poisoning in horses and cows), so is subject to legislation in the UK and should not be grown near paddocks or grazing .

THE MAGIC OF RAGWORT
In Ireland, it was believed that fairies and witches used its stems as their broomsticks, so was called 'fairies' horse'. It was said that if you pulled up ragwort, you had to apologize to it or else the fairies would get you.

pollinator

Uses GROW RAGWORT TO ENCOURAGE BEES AND OTHER INSECTS, INCLUDING THE BLACK AND RED CINNABAR MOTH.

🧺 SEPTEMBER ONWARDS

🌱 JULY TO OCTOBER

🟫 SEPTEMBER DIRECTLY WHERE THEY ARE TO FLOWER. ON LIGHT, LOW-FERTILITY SOIL

↕ 90CM (2FT 11IN)

29 CHAMOMILE

P (MATRICARIA CHAMOMILLA)
★ *also known as ground apple, whig plant, maythen*

The pretty daisy-like flowers of chamomile grow close to the ground and smell a little like apple, hence its common name, 'ground apple'. It can be grown as a lawn, and there is nowhere lovelier to be than lying on a patch of chamomile on a summer's day. A more attainable way to cultivate it, however, is from seed in a pot, which it takes to very well, or to scatter it where you wish it to grow. Although it is an annual, it self-seeds abundantly, guaranteeing fresh blooms the following year.

Uses USE DRIED FLOWERS IN A POTPOURRI MIX TO ADD THE SCENT OF APPLES. ADD A SPOONFUL OF HONEY TO CHAMOMILE TEA FOR A SOOTHING, LATE-NIGHT DRINK.

Chamomile has long been regarded as a healing and cosmetic plant. It's the flowers you want – pick them when the petals turn back, any time from Midsummer Day until the end of August. The soothing power of chamomile tea is well known and it is considered a mild sedative if drunk before going to sleep. Also try it as a rinse for fair hair, a soothing eye bath or a face wash, to keep skin soft and supple.

SOW IN A POT

THE MAGIC OF CHAMOMILE
Chamomile is associated with resilience and can soothe those experiencing a hard time and needing support. Planted over a grave, it is said to calm a restless spirit (and create a bee-friendly blanket). More cheerfully, a bath scattered with chamomile flowers is said to attract love.

WHEN FLOWERS HAVE DIED BACK AND THE CENTRAL CONE IS DRY

SPRING AND SUMMER

30CM (12IN)

LATE SPRING, DIRECTLY WHERE THEY ARE TO FLOWER

30 HYSSOP

(HYSSOPUS OFFICINALIS)
★ *also known as isopo, hyssop herb*

SHAKE SEEDS
FROM THE DRIED
FLOWERS

Looking and tasting a little like lavender, hyssop has woody stems, pungent, pointy leaves and spikes of blue or deep pink flowers that bloom for a long time. It is easy and rewarding to grow and, once established, self-seeds readily. An ancient herb, hyssop is mentioned in the Bible: 'Purge me with hyssop, and I shall be clean.' (Psalm 51.7, *New Revised Standard Version*). Its name derives from the Hebrew 'ezob' which translates as 'holy herb'.

THE MAGIC OF HYSSOP

Hyssop is used magically to purify and cleanse, not just physically but also psychically and mentally. Scatter or sprinkle some on yourself or in the bath when you want rid of unpleasant people or experiences or to battle against dark moods. Hildegard of Bingen, the medieval physician, recommended chicken cooked in hyssop and wine as a treatment for sadness.

Uses THE LEAVES HAVE A FRESH, MINTY TASTE — ADD TO SALADS, SPRINKLE OVER PASTA DISHES OR WHEN POACHING STONE FRUIT, SUCH AS PEACHES OR APRICOTS.

WHEN THE FLOWER SPIKES HAVE TURNED BROWN, SNIP OFF THE ENTIRE FLOWER AND SHAKE SEEDS OUT ONTO PAPER OR INTO A CONTAINER TO DRY

SPRING, DIRECTLY WHERE THEY ARE TO FLOWER, IN LIGHT, WELL-DRAINED SOIL IN A SUNNY SPOT AFTER LAST FROSTS

AUGUST TO OCTOBER

UP TO 60CM (2FT)

THE JOY OF COMPOST

Compost is nature's way of dealing with its own waste, and it is magical. You take a load of unwanted vegetable peelings and garden detritus, heap them up and, with a little care and attention, they turn into a wonderful, dark brown, organic material that you can use to improve the soil and feed your plants in your veg plot or flower beds. The ideal – perhaps the dream – compost set-up is three or four bins in a row. As each bin fills up, it is turned over into the next. This introduces oxygen into the compost, which helps to speed up decomposition. Most of us don't have room for that many bins, but I have found one bin works just fine.

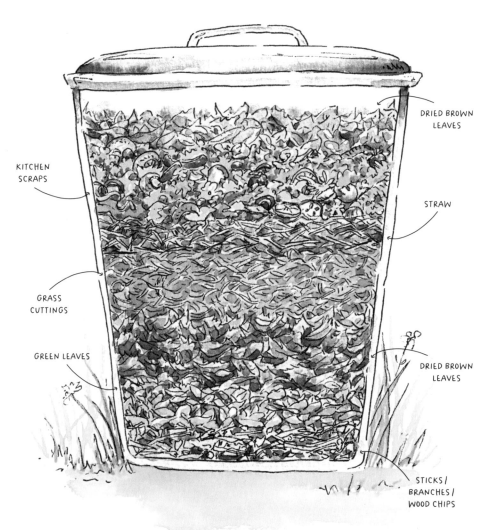

DRIED BROWN
LEAVES

KITCHEN
SCRAPS

STRAW

GRASS
CUTTINGS

GREEN LEAVES

DRIED BROWN
LEAVES

STICKS /
BRANCHES /
WOOD CHIPS

THE BEST WAY TO GET GOOD RESULTS
You need the right combination of materials containing carbon and nitrogen:

★ dry, brown materials, such as cardboard and dry leaves, for the carbon
★ organic green matter, such as vegetable scraps, grass cuttings and plant prunings, for the nitrogen.

Cut or shred everything into smaller pieces. That will help to speed up the decomposition.

Don't add meat, fish, dairy products or cat and dog droppings. That will make the compost stink. Restrict what you add to simply plant materials.

Turn the compost every so often to introduce oxygen so the bacteria can get to work.

KITCHEN SCRAPS

BOKASHI BRAN

BOKASHI BIN

If you don't have space for even a single compost heap, consider a bokashi composting system, which you can keep in the kitchen This Japanese method involves layering all kitchen scraps in a bin with a special bran and covering tightly. When full, it is sealed shut for 10 to 14 days, every other day draining the liquid off via a tap on the bucket. The waste is fermented and pickled in this time, creating a mush that can be added to fallow soil (it will remain acidic for about a month), and the liquid drained off can be diluted and used as a fertilizer.

31 ◀ RUE

🌱 (*RUTA GRAVEOLENS*)
★ also known as herb of grace, herbygrass

Rue is not a popular herb these days, possibly because, as the '*graveolens*' in its Latin name tells us, it has 'an offensive smell', bitter taste and it can irritate the skin. That's a shame as it is attractive, with fern-like leaves and pretty yellow flowers, and butterflies love it. It also has a fascinating history. Roman herbalist Pliny lauded it in his *Natural History*, but don't take his advice to steal it from another's garden for best results. Also, reportedly, Michelangelo and Leonardo da Vinci chewed it to improve their eyesight, but don't try this yourself.

bitter taste

SEEDS

THE MAGIC OF RUE
Rue was cited as a witch's herb during the witch trials in southern England in the seventeenth century. If a woman grew it, she was condemned as a witch. Now, it has a more cheerful association: it is used to stuff poppets (fabric figures representing particular people) when doing healing work or to protect those within a circle before practising magic.

Uses MUSLIN POUCHES FILLED WITH RUE OR DRIED BUNCHES HUNG UP CAN BE USED TO DETER MOSQUITOES AND FLEAS. WEAR GLOVES WHEN HANDLING RUE, THOUGH, AS IT CAN IRRITATE THE SKIN.

🧺 LATE SUMMER, AFTER FLOWERING, WHEN SEED CAPSULES TURN BROWN

NEED A TEMPERATURE OF 20°C AND CAN TAKE 4 WEEKS TO GERMINATE

🌱 MARCH, IN SEED TRAYS, OR IN APRIL, DIRECTLY WHERE THEY ARE TO FLOWER, IN A SUNNY SPOT. SEEDS

🌷 JULY TO OCTOBER

↕🌱 UP TO 70CM (2FT 3½IN)

32 SAGE

(SALVIA OFFICINALIS)

★ *also known as red sage, garden sage, sawge*

This easy-to-grow herb is a familiar sight and taste to anyone with even the mildest interest in herbs. Its leaves, which it keeps all year, are narrow, pointed and a greyish-green, accompanied by pale violet flowers on long spikes that rise above the foliage in autumn.

Sage's Latin name '*Salvia*' means 'to be well' or 'to save', which is a reference to the plant's healing properties. It was widely used in the early days of medicine to steady the nerves, soothe throat infections and ease digestive problems. Indeed, a cup of sage tea is supposed to settle the stomach after a big meal. It can also prevent night sweats and excessive perspiration. Chewing or mashing up a leaf and applying it to a bite or sting takes away the itch.

COLLECT SEEDS IN SEPTEMBER

THE MAGIC OF SAGE

Sage has an ancient reputation for warding off evil, 'dispelling of evil spyrites', and for working 'agaynst the biting of serpents'. It also makes frequent appearances in love spells.

SEPTEMBER, WHEN FLOWERS BEGIN TO TURN BROWN AND SEEDS ARE DARK

SPRING, DIRECTLY WHERE THEY ARE TO GROW, AFTER LAST FROSTS, OR SOW IN SEED TRAYS IN MARCH

JULY TO OCTOBER

UP TO 1.2M (3FT 11IN), DEPENDING ON VARIETY

Uses TRY ADDING A FEW LEAVES TO WARM APPLE JUICE TO GIVE IT A SATISFYINGLY EARTHY FLAVOUR. SAGE'S CULINARY USES ARE MANY, FROM SAGE AND ONION STUFFING TO SAUSAGES AND CREAMY PASTA DISHES. IT CAN ALSO BE USED AS A NATURAL HAIR TONIC, GENERALLY ADDING BOUNCE AND SHINE, AND FOR DARKENING GREY HAIRS.

33 SWEET WOODRUFF

P *(GALIUM ODORATUM)*
★ *also known as sweet-scented bedstraw*

vanilla scent

Although a modest, ground-hugging plant, sweet woodruff surprises, with its new shoots appearing before most other plants in spring, particularly when growing under a tree. Its pretty white flowers follow in summer. The leaves of sweet woodruff have a pleasing scent, so during the Middle Ages, they were strewn on the floor of 'my lady's chamber' to sweeten the air, hence its folk name of 'sweet-scented bedstraw'.

Sweet woodruff is easy to grow from seed, but it is even easier to propagate by dividing a clump and transplanting. It will happily settle into a new patch.

LARGE
SEED PODS

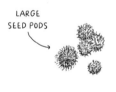

THE MAGIC OF SWEET WOODRUFF
It was believed that a posy hung over a cot blessed the baby and kept it safe.

Uses WHEN CUT, SWEET WOODRUFF FLOWERS RELEASE A VANILLA SCENT THAT, WHEN DRIED, WORKS WELL IN POTPOURRIS (SEE PAGE 84). IT WAS TUCKED INTO LINEN TO KEEP MOTHS AND OTHER INSECTS OFF, SO THAT'S WORTH A TRY TOO.

🧺 JULY, AUGUST, WHEN FULLY RIPE

◆ EARLY SPRING, DIRECTLY WHERE THEY ARE TO FLOWER

🌷 APRIL AND MAY

↕🌱 UP TO 30CM (12IN)

34 ROSEMARY

🌱 *(SALVIA ROSMARINUS)*
★ *also known as the dew of the sea, Mary's mantle, pilgrim's flower, compass weed*

A fragrant, evergreen shrub with small blue flowers and distinctive stiff, narrow leaves, rosemary is easy to grow and withstands most conditions. One of the most recognizable and useful plants, it has many magical uses, appearing in countless charms, spells and traditions. It is holy, too. It is said that the flowers were white until Mary spread Jesus' clothes to dry on a rosemary bush during the flight to Egypt, and then they turned blue. Later, it came to represent immortality and remembrance, so was carried at funerals and thrown into coffins.

easy to grow

SEEDS TAKE THREE WEEKS TO GERMINATE

THE MAGIC OF ROSEMARY
Among the many supposed powers of rosemary are its ability to keep ghosts, thieves and witches away from the home. A box made of rosemary and sniffed daily has the unlikely outcome of bestowing immortality on the sniffer. It is said that a gardener who plants rosemary will never be without friends.

🧺 SUMMER, ONCE THE FLOWERS BEGIN TO TURN BROWN AND DRY

🌑 IN SPRING, DIRECTLY WHERE THEY ARE TO GROW, IN A SUNNY,

SHELTERED SPOT. SEEDS TAKE ABOUT 3 WEEKS TO GERMINATE

🌱 APRIL AND MAY

↕🌱 UP TO 1.5M (4FT 11IN)

Uses A ROSEMARY FOOT BATH IS REFRESHING FOR TIRED FEET AFTER A LONG WALK. MAKE ENOUGH ROSEMARY DECOCTION (SEE PAGE 104) TO COVER YOUR FEET WHEN PLACED IN A BOWL. ALLOW TO COOL TO A COMFORTABLE TEMPERATURE, THEN SOAK FEET LEISURELY. TO RELIEVE A HEAD COLD, FILL A MUSLIN BAG WITH FRESH, CRUSHED ROSEMARY AND LEMON VERBENA LEAVES AND HOLD UNDER THE NOSE.

35 ◁ FEVERFEW

🌿 *(TANACETUM PARTHENIUM, SYNONYM: CHRYSANTHEMUM PARTHENIUM)*
★ *also known as batchelor's buttons, nosebleed, midsummer daisy*

Feverfew's small, white, daisy-like flowers with their prominent yellow centres are easily mistaken for chamomile. Unlike chamomile, however, the flowers are not attractive to bees and other pollinators because of their pungent scent. All parts of the plant are strongly aromatic, and the scent grows stronger when dried.

This plant has been used as a painkiller since ancient Greek and Roman times, and was later cultivated in monastery gardens. Known as the housewife's aspirin, it is credited with being a remedy for various ailments, including headaches, menstrual pain, fevers, toothache, even as a cure for melancholy.

THE MAGIC OF FEVERFEW
Feverfew can be used if a person is hit by an arrow dispatched by an invisible fairy. Such a stabbing pain, known as 'elf shot', is more likely to be muscle cramp or a stitch, however, which feverfew is unlikely to assuage.

strongly aromatic

Uses FILL A BOWL WITH DRIED FEVERFEW FLOWERS TO REPEL INSECTS. A TISANE OF FLOWERS IS A REMEDY FOR A HEADACHE OR A MIGRAINE.

🧺 OCTOBER, AFTER FLOWERING, WHEN THE SEED HEADS ARE DRY

🌱 JULY TO OCTOBER

↕🌱 UP TO 50CM (1FT 8IN)

◆ SPRING, SOWING THE FINE SEEDS THINLY, DIRECTLY WHERE THEY ARE TO FLOWER

36 OAK

(QUERCUS)

★ also known as white oak, Jove's nuts, dair (Irish)

The oak is synonymous with strength and steadfastness. Its paw-shaped leaves, gnarly bark and outspread branches greet you like open arms, having the familiarity of an old and valued friend. Its long life, presence in the forest and usefulness as a source of fuel, shelter and timber, have justifiably earned it the title 'king of the forest', given to it by the Druids, who continue to venerate it.

The oak is also one of the most important plants in folklore, with myths and legends associated with it worldwide and spanning centuries. It was venerated by Greek, Roman, Celtic, Slavic and Teutonic nations, and associated with their most powerful gods – Zeus (Greeks), Jupiter (Romans), Dagda (Irish), Perun (Slavs) and Thor (Norse). The classical world also regarded it as the tree of life, connecting heaven and earth, with its deep roots penetrating into the underworld and its branches soaring towards the sky.

king of the forest

THE MAGIC OF THE OAK

Rainwater collected in hollows of an oak tree was once used to treat a fever, inflamed gums, wounds and eczema. An acorn grated into custard was given as a treatment for diarrhoea. An American folk remedy was to boil oak leaves that had stayed on a tree over winter and soak frostbitten limbs in the cooled liquid for an hour a day for a week to cure frostbite. A wand made from an oak branch is said to heighten its user's magical powers.

Uses ACORNS CAN BE MADE INTO A REASONABLE COFFEE SUBSTITUTE. DRY, BAKE, THEN GRIND THE ACORNS AND USE AS YOU WOULD INSTANT COFFEE.

🧺 AUTUMN, AFTER A STRONG WIND

 IN A POT, SOON AFTER COLLECTING. ACORNS GERMINATE EASILY AND NEED LITTLE ATTENTION; KEEP MOIST AND PROTECT FROM MICE

POT ON AS SEEDLINGS GROW INTO SAPLINGS AND PLANT OUT WHEN 2M (6FT 6IN) TALL

 45M (150FT) WHEN MATURE, BUT TAKES 100 YEARS

DEVIL'S BIT SCABIOUS

(SUCCISA PRATENSIS, SYNONYM: SCABIOSA SUCCISA)
★ *also known as Bobby bright buttons, blue bonnets, blue ball*

Happiest growing along a riverbank or in a damp meadow, where its domes of tiny flowers float on tender stems like a purpley-blue haze, Devil's bit scabious is pollen-rich and loved by bees and butterflies. If you have poor soil that is otherwise tricky to find plants for, it's perfect as, though it will grow in a fertile garden, it becomes bigger and not so dainty and appealing.

THE MAGIC OF DEVIL'S BIT SCABIOUS

Legend has it that the intriguing part of the name of this plant, 'Devil's bit', comes from its stumpy black root, truncated by the Devil, who was envious of its ability to heal, specifically skin conditions such as scabies and the sores of bubonic plague. The word 'scabies' comes from the Latin *'scabere'*, 'to scratch'.

Uses THE MOST SIGNIFICANT USE FOR DEVIL'S BIT SCABIOUS IS AS A NECTAR-SOURCE FOR POLLINATORS, ESPECIALLY HOVERFLIES. THE LARVAE OF MARSH FRITILLARY BUTTERFLIES ALSO FEAST ON ITS NECTAR. IT IS ALSO STILL USED IN HERBAL MEDICINES TO TREAT ECZEMA, AND OTHER SKIN COMPLAINTS, AND IN AN INFUSION TO EASE COUGHS AND FEVERS.

🧺 AUTUMN, WHEN FLOWER HEADS ARE DRY AND BROWN

🌱 JULY TO OCTOBER

↕🌱 UP TO 1M (3FT 3IN)

MARCH OR APRIL, DIRECTLY WHERE THEY ARE TO FLOWER

38 ▸ HERB ROBERT

🌿 *(GERANIUM ROBERTIANUM)*
★ *also known as death-comes-quickly, stinking Robert, squinter-pip, granny-thread-the-needle*

You can find this wild flower peeping out from woodland edges or tucked into a shady wall. It grows vigorously and its five-petalled, star-shaped pink flowers appear from May to September. Its hairiness and unpleasant smell when rubbed between the fingers has earned it one of its names, stinking Robert.

THE MAGIC OF HERB ROBERT

When grown outdoors, herb Robert was said to bring good luck, but if you took it indoors, death was sure to follow. The plant is associated, and possibly named after, Robin Goodfellow, a cheeky trickster goblin who loved to play practical jokes, including shape-shifting to confuse people. Like the plant, he was hairy, red-featured and carried a candlestick – the plant's seed pods are long and pointed and sit in their calyx like a candle in a holder.

Uses THE FLOWERING STEMS OF HERB ROBERT CAN BE USED IN AN INFUSION TO CHECK NOSE BLEEDS AND TO TREAT DIARRHOEA AND OTHER STOMACH UPSETS. CHOPPED FRESH LEAVES SOOTHE SKIN DISORDERS, BOILS AND HEAL SEPTIC WOUNDS. A DECOCTION CAN BE USED AS A GARGLE FOR TONSILITIS.

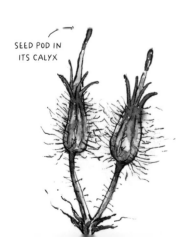

SEED POD IN
ITS CALYX

🧺 SEPTEMBER TO OCTOBER, BUT SELF-SEEDS FREELY

🌱 SPRING DIRECTLY WHERE THEY ARE TO FLOWER

🌷 MAY TO SEPTEMBER

↕🌱 UP TO 40CM (1FT 3IN)

DRYING FLOWERS AND SEED HEADS

If they are dried carefully, seed heads and flowers will continue to look lovely all through the winter. Drying them is not difficult but well worth taking a little care over.

THE BEST WAY TO DRY SEED HEADS
1. Cut off the seed heads,* keeping a good length of stem.

2. Put into a paper bag, with the seed head at the bottom, but not touching the bag, and close with a rubber band or string around the stems.

3. Hang the bag up until the seeds fall out. Remove the bag and collect the seeds. You will be left with empty, skeletal seed heads to display in your best vase.

You can also dry grasses this way.

*The exception is the seedheads of Love-in-a-mist *(Nigella)* which are best picked when green as this keeps their colour and form. If you want to collect the seed, leave a few to dry until they rattle, then shake out the seed.

Two ways to dry flowers

AIR DRY

This is a similar method to drying seed heads and grasses, but without the paper bag.

1. Collect bunches of a single species of flowers. Restrict your bunches to six or seven blooms.

2. Tie near the base with string and hang upside down in a cool place for at least two weeks.

3. When the petals rustle, they are ready. Some people spray with hairspray to protect them, but this is not really necessary.

Good for: larkspur, lavender, achillea, roses, cornflowers, hydrangeas.

PUT IN A FLOWER PRESS

A bought or ready-made flower press consists of two pieces of wood that can be tightened with wing nuts, compressing flowers between sheets of paper.

Alternatively, simply put the flowers between pieces of paper (smooth white is best) weighted down with heavy books.

1. Remove any unwanted leaves from the flower stems.

2. Place the flowers carefully between two sheets of paper, taking care that the flowers do not touch one another.

3. Either tighten the wing nuts on a flower press or pile a couple of heavy books on top.

4. Leave for two or three weeks and resist the temptation to look. If you do peek, you could rip the flowers.

Good for: borage, larkspur, verbena, pansies, zinnias, delphiniums.

EYEBRIGHT

🌱 *(EUPHRASIA OFFICINALIS)*
★ *also known as casse-lunettes, peewits, clear-eye, fairy flax*

A beauty in miniature, eyebright has small white flowers with purple stripes, a bright orange patch at the throat and a dark centre. Looking a little like a wide-open eye, it is an example of the age old concept of the 'doctrine of signatures', which is that plants look like the parts of the body they are to treat, so it has been used to treat eye complaints for centuries.

Although it grows happily in the wild, it is harder to cultivate in the garden, as its roots feed on nearby plants and it only grows in grass. Once it has become established, however, allow its tiny seeds, held in heart-shaped pods, to disperse and it will come back year after year.

If you need any more reasons to love this delightful plant, its Latin name, '*Euphrasia*', derives from 'Euphrosyne', Greek goddess of joy and mirth.

THE MAGIC OF EYEBRIGHT
An infusion applied gently to the eyelids could aid clairvoyance. Carried, it is credited with increasing psychic powers.

HEART-SHAPED
SEED PODS

Uses TO SOOTHE TIRED OR INFLAMED EYES, BATHE THEM WITH EYEBRIGHT INFUSED IN WARM STERILISED WATER.

 OCTOBER

AUTUMN, DIRECTLY WHERE IT IS TO FLOWER, IN A SUNNY, GRASSY SPOT, OR KEEP REFRIGERATED FOR 90 DAYS, AS NEED TO BE CHILLED

TO BREAK DORMANCY AND TRIGGER GERMINATION IN SPRING

 LATE SUMMER

10 TO 15CM (4 TO 6IN)

GREAT YELLOW GENTIAN

🌱 *(GENTIANA LUTEA)*

★ *also known as bitter root, yellow gentian, hochwurzel*

It takes dedication and a sense of purpose to grow great yellow gentian from seed. Germination time is lengthy, and the plant can take ten years to flower. When it does, though, you will be rewarded with whorls of showy golden flowers clustered among the leaves on tall stems. (This plant is not to be confused with the more recognizable blue or purplish blue gentian.) The many winged seeds that follow are encased in a long, upright capsule. It's the reputed health benefits of the plant that make its cultivation worthwhile: it is regarded as one of the best herbal tonics.

THE MAGIC OF GREAT YELLOW GENTIAN
It can be sprinkled into baths or added to sachets to attract love. It has also been used to break curses and hexes.

winged seeds

Uses DRIED ROOTS OF ESTABLISHED PLANTS CAN BE PREPARED AS AN INFUSION TO EASE DIGESTIVE AND MENSTRUAL PROBLEMS AND TACKLE COLDS. ADD HALF A TEASPOON OF ROOT TO A CUP OF HOT WATER, AND STEEP FOR 10 MINUTES BEFORE DRINKING. THE BITTER TASTE CAN BE SWEETENED WITH HONEY.

🧺 SEPTEMBER, OCTOBER. IT IS A PROTECTED SPECIES SO BUY SEEDS FIRST, THEN HARVEST FROM THEM, RATHER THAN COLLECT IN THE WILD

🔶 AUTUMN, DIRECTLY WHERE THEY ARE TO FLOWER, IN A SUNNY SPOT

🌱 JUNE TO AUGUST

↕🌱 UP TO 1.5M (4FT 11IN)

41 ◄ HOLLY

🌱 🌑 *(ILEX AQUIFOLIUM)*
★ *also known as bat's wings, Christ's thorn, holy tree, holm*

Evergreen, with barbed, glossy leaves and shiny red berries, holly is one of the most recognizable plants; it is also one of the most magical. Countless legends and lore are attributed to it. To Christians, the spiky leaves and red berries symbolize Christ's crown of thorns and his blood, so represent eternal life. To Druids, the Holly King represents winter and fought at the turn of the seasons with the Oak King for rulership of the year ahead. To pagans, traditionally, holly was regarded as masculine so could only be brought into the house by a man.

THE MAGIC OF HOLLY

A holly tree outside a house is said to bring good luck and protect the occupants from lightning, storms and fires, especially if it self-seeded. People would throw a sprig of holly in the direction an animal went as it was thought to have the power to make animals return. A wand made from a holly branch brings protection to whoever uses it to practise magic.

🧺 NOVEMBER AND DECEMBER, WHEN THE BERRIES ARE RIPE

🔶 SOAK BERRIES IN WARM WATER FOR SEVERAL DAYS TO SOFTEN THE FLESH, THEN SQUASH IN A SIEVE TO EXTRACT THE SEEDS. MIX EQUAL PARTS HORTICULTURAL GRIT AND COMPOST IN A BUCKET. LAY THE SEEDS ON TOP, COVER WITH SAND AND LEAVE FOR 18 MONTHS (THE SEEDS HAVE A HARD OUTER COAT AND TAKE A WHILE TO BREAK DOWN). IN SPRING, SOW IN POTS TO ESTABLISH BEFORE PLANTING OUTSIDE

🌱 EARLY SPRING TO THE START OF SUMMER

↕🌱 UP TO 15M (50FT)

Uses THE ANCIENT ROMANS GATHERED HOLLY AND BROUGHT IT INSIDE TO DECORATE THEIR HOMES AS PART OF THEIR SATURNALIA CELEBRATIONS IN DECEMBER. A GOOD IDEA TO COPY! MAKE A WREATH OR A FESTIVE TABLE DECORATION WITH HOLLY TO BRING THIS MAGIC PLANT INTO THE HOUSE AT YULE. KEEP THE SPRIG FROM THE TOP OF THE CHRISTMAS PUDDING, THEN BURN WITH SOME NEW LEAVES AS A CHARM OF CONTINUITY

42 WILD CHERRY

🌿 *(PRUNUS AVIUM)*
★ *also known as sweet cherry, bird cherry, hagberry, Suffolk merries*

The burst of pure-white blossom on a cherry tree in spring feels miraculous after the dark days of winter. Little wonder that it is wreathed in folklore, customs and magic. In Japan, the short-flowering time of the cherry (one week) is acknowledged during sakura hanami (cherry blossom viewing) where it symbolizes the fleeting nature of life. Cherry blossom is also the flower of the samurai warrior, representing their brief but glorious existence.

In Scotland, the cherry was once considered to be the witches' tree – anyone felling a tree to use the wood would be cursed.

Uses

THE FRUIT OF THE WILD CHERRY IS TOO SOUR AND INDIGESTIBLE TO EAT, BUT DOES MAKE AN EXCELLENT CHERRY BRANDY. MIX EQUAL PARTS CHERRIES, SUGAR AND BRANDY. POUR INTO A BOTTLE AND LEAVE FOR A FEW MONTHS.

The froth of white blossom in the spring is followed by small, shiny red/purple cherries with the stones (seeds) inside, followed by the leaves turning orange and red in the autumn. Cherry stones have long been used for divination: you may remember the rhyme 'Tinker, Tailor, Soldier, Sailor, Rich Man, Poor Man, Beggar Man, Thief', where cherry stones were cast and counted to foretell future careers or husbands.

THE MAGIC OF CHERRIES

To attract love, try a Japanese custom of tying a single strand of your hair to a blossoming cherry tree. To find out how many years you will live, run around a tree full of ripe cherries, then shake it. The number that fall represent the number of years you have left.

🧺 JULY, WHEN CHERRIES ARE ALMOST BLACK

 FIRST, CLEAN THE CHERRY STONES. THEN MIX WITH HORTICULTURAL SAND AND COMPOST (ONE HANDFUL OF CHERRIES TO TWO HANDFULS OF MIXTURE). COVER WITH SAND AND LEAVE IN A BUCKET IN A SHADY SPOT. SOW SEEDS IN FEBRUARY, DIRECTLY WHERE THEY ARE TO GROW

🌷 APRIL

↕🌱 18 TO 25M (60 TO 80FT)

43 AGRIMONY

LEAF

🌱 *(AGRIMONIA EUPATORIA)*

★ *also known as sticklewort, liverwort*

You may come across this tall plant with its spikes of yellow flowers as you walk along country lanes – it thrives in hedgerows, on road verges and field margins. In cities, it can also be found on wasteland.

Long regarded as a medicinal plant, its common name, agrimony, is thought to come from the Greek word *'agremone'*, which was used for plants that supposedly healed cataracts. Agrimony has been used to treat catarrh, digestive problems and liver and kidney disorders. It can also be used as a natural dye: all parts of the plant produce a strong yellow colour. Look out for it from July to September, when it flowers, and harvest it when the sun is shining – it is a herb of the sun in Leo.

seed head

🧺 SEPTEMBER TO OCTOBER

🔶 SEEDS CAN BE TRICKY TO GERMINATE. FOR BEST RESULTS, MIX WITH A LITTLE VERMICULITE AND PUT IN A PLASTIC BAG IN THE FRIDGE FOR 6 WEEKS OR SO. ONCE GERMINATED, SOW IN SOME POTTING COMPOST

🌷 JULY TO SEPTEMBER

↕🌱 UP TO IM (3FT 3IN)

Uses COMMON AGRIMONY WAS USED IN SPELLS TO PROTECT AGAINST EVIL AND MISFORTUNE. TAKE AGRIMONY TO SLIP INTO A DEEP AND RESTFUL SLEEP. EITHER SPRINKLE SOME FLOWERS AND LEAVES BENEATH YOUR PILLOW OR DUNK IN A TEAPOT WITH HOT WATER TO MAKE A CALMING INFUSION.

44 BETONY

ₚ (STACHYS OFFICINALIS)
★ also known as wood betony, hedge nettle, lousewort, sentinel of the woods

Betony is a perennial herb that can be found growing in woods, hedges, heaths and moors. Look for its reddish-purple flowers, which grow in whorls on spikes.

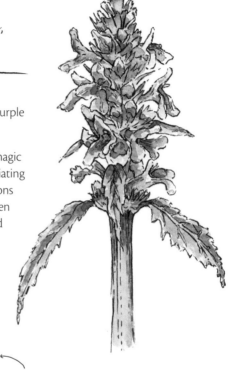

Once considered a remedy for all ills and a magic plant, betony has been credited with alleviating a huge number of conditions. Concoctions made from its flowering stems have been used as a remedy for anxiety, panic and depression, easing headaches and hysteria, treating diarrhoea, cystitis, asthma and calming neuralgia. Drinking an infusion made from a few leaves is certainly invigorating.

seed head

SEEDS

THE MAGIC OF BETONY

Betony has long been associated with magic and superstition. In medieval Germany, a witch was identified as 'she who digs up the betony', and it was planted in graveyards to keep ghost activity to a minimum. It was also thought to be a cure for the mysterious-sounding 'elf sickness'.

Uses PLACE A FEW LEAVES AND FLOWERS UNDER YOUR PILLOW IF YOU SUFFER FROM BAD DREAMS OR VISIONS. THERE IS ALSO A MIDSUMMER TRADITION OF BURNING IT ON A BONFIRE AND JUMPING THROUGH THE SMOKE TO PURIFY THE BODY OF ILLS AND EVILS.

🧺 SEPTEMBER, WHEN FLOWER HEADS ARE DRY

🌷 JULY TO AUGUST

↕ UP TO 60CM (2FT)

◆ SPRING OR LATE SUMMER, DIRECTLY WHERE THEY ARE TO FLOWER

45 ▷ WHITE CLOVER

ℙ (TRIFOLIUM REPENS)
★ *also known as honey, honeystalks, shamrock, trefoil*

Once seen as a weed and driven from lawns with herbicide, clover is now recognized as a nectar- and nitrogen-rich plant to be valued. There is a growing trend to sow clover lawns, which keep bees and pollinators happy and results in a snowy field of white flowers underfoot in summer. A perennial herb, it is common in meadows and fields and farmers cultivate it as animal fodder or plough it back in to enrich the soil. It has three-lobed leaves (apart from exceptions, see below), with globe-like flower heads that bear fruit containing two seeds in a pod, which springs open to disperse them.

nectar-rich

THE MAGIC OF CLOVER

Traditionally, it's a four-leaved clover that is the one to look out for. That's because they are attributed with no end of amazing powers, from general good luck to detecting fairies and bringing a separated lover home safely. As one old rhyme puts it:

I'll seek a four-leaved clover
In all the fairy dells
And if I find the charmed leaf
Oh how I'll weave my spells

Even rarer is a five-leaved clover, said to powerfully attract money.

🧺 OCTOBER

🌷 JUNE TO SEPTEMBER

 SPRING, DIRECTLY WHERE THEY ARE TO GROW, WHEN THE DANGER OF FROST HAS PASSED, AS NEED WARMTH TO GERMINATE. SOW THE TINY SEEDS THINLY

 5 TO 20CM (2 TO 8IN)

Uses CLOVER HAS MANY USES IN HERBAL MEDICINE AND IS CREDITED WITH BEING AN ASTRINGENT, EXPECTORANT AND WITH HEALING WOUNDS. THE FRESH YOUNG LEAVES ARE GOOD ADDED TO A SALAD OR COOKED AND EATEN LIKE SPINACH.

MISTLETOE

(VISCUM ALBUM)
★ also known as all heal, holy wood, witches' broom, birdlime

The pearl-like, translucent berries of mistletoe come to light in winter when their host trees lose their leaves. Clustered among shiny, green leaves, which sprout directly from the bark, it's a magical-looking plant. It grows on apple trees, so is often seen in orchards. Its seeds are mostly spread by birds, which eat the berries, depositing the sticky seeds on tree branches by wiping them from their beaks or in their droppings.

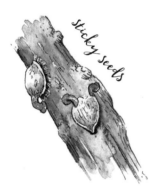

sticky seeds

THE MAGIC OF MISTLETOE

Some examples of folklore include these. It was placed in cradles to prevent children from being stolen by fairies and replaced with changelings. A ring of carved mistletoe wood wards off sickness. When carried, it will cure fresh wounds quickly and bring good luck in hunting. When burnt, it will banish evil. Worn around the neck it will make the wearer invisible

NOTE: THERE IS LOTS OF CONFLICTING ADVICE ABOUT GROWING MISTLETOE FROM SEED. THOUGH NOT THAT HARD, IT TAKES PATIENCE: ONLY 1 IN 10 SEEDS GERMINATES AND FIRST TRUE LEAVES APPEAR IN THIRD YEAR

FEBRUARY, MARCH OR APRIL, COLLECT FRESH BERRIES. SOW IMMEDIATELY BY SQUEEZING A SEED OUT AND 'PLANTING' IT AS HIGH UP AS POSSIBLE ON A TREE BRANCH (APPLE, POPLAR, LIME OR HAWTHORN ARE GOOD), BY INSERTING IT INTO A CREVICE OR CUTTING A NOTCH WITH A SMALL FLAP TO COVER IT. 'SOW' AT LEAST 20 SEEDS, COVERING WITH HESSIAN TO PROTECT FROM BIRDS. GERMINATION SHOULD HAVE TAKEN PLACE BY APRIL

Uses ALTHOUGH PROBABLY NOT FATAL, THE BERRIES ARE TOXIC, SO DO NOT EAT THEM. INSTEAD, ADD SPRIGS TO A CHRISTMAS WREATH OR HANG SOME OVER A DOORWAY. KISS YOUR LOVED ONE UNDER MISTLETOE, IT IS SAID, AND YOUR LOVE WILL REMAIN TRUE.

GARDENING BY THE MOON

'Plant the bean when the moon is light, plant potatoes when the moon is dark.' Old saying

The gravitational pull of the moon is the main cause of the tides, and high tide is due to the oceans facing the moon bulging in response to this pull. Some gardeners believe the moon also influences plant growth and adjust their planting and the sowing of seeds accordingly.

As the moon affects all water on Earth, it affects the sap in plants. The sap rises when the moon waxes (becomes full), and falls when it wanes (diminishes). At a new moon, water is pulled up through the soil, causing seeds to swell. As it waxes, its gravitational pull helps root growth, so this is a good time to plant root crops and to transplant seedlings. As the moon wanes, the pull lessens, making this the best time to harvest crops and to prune.

The moon is also thought to affect plant growth through geotropism – that is, gravity encourages roots to grow downwards and stems upwards.

The four phases of the moon

PHASE ONE: between a new moon and the first quarter. Time to plant leafy crops.

PHASE TWO: between the first quarter and a full moon. Time to plant fruit crops.

PHASE THREE: between a full moon and the last quarter. Time to plant root crops and perennials.

PHASE FOUR: between the last quarter and a new moon. A good time to prune and weed. As the moon is waning, the water table is receding, so it is not a good time for planting.

A journal showing the phases of the moon will help you to plan and manage lunar gardening.

47 ⚑ MARSH MALLOW

🌱 *(ALTHAEA OFFICINALIS)*
★ also known as Joseph's staff, mortification root, wymot

This hardy perennial is happiest growing in marshy ground (hence its name) or near the coast. It has soft, velvety, grey-green leaves and pale pink, open flowers that bloom from mid summer to early autumn. The root was once used to thicken sweets that came to be called marshmallows, but is no longer used for this purpose.

COLLECT SEEDS IN AUTUMN

THE MAGIC OF MARSH MALLOW

If your lover has left you, leave a vase of marsh mallows outside your door. This is said to make your ex think of you and possibly return.

Uses THE ROOT OF THE MARSH MALLOW IS VALUED IN FOLK MEDICINE FOR ITS HEALING AND SOOTHING PROPERTIES AND FOR TREATING CHEST COMPLAINTS. TAP ROOTS, HARVESTED IN AUTUMN FROM PLANTS AT LEAST TWO YEARS OLD, CAN BE COOKED AND EATEN. THEY TASTE A LITTLE LIKE PARSNIPS.

 WHEN SEED PODS ARE COMPLETELY DRY

🌷 JULY TO SEPTEMBER

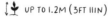 AS SOON AS SEEDS ARE RIPE IN LATE SUMMER

↕🌱 UP TO 1.2M (3FT 11IN)

48 ▷ TEASEL

🌱 *(DIPSACUS FULLONUM)*
★ *also known as Venus's basin, barber's brushes, donkey's thistle*

The memorable name of this spiny and handsome plant comes from the fact that birds, especially goldfinches, tease the seeds from its seed heads with their beaks. In fact, the plant provides them with a buffet, as water collects at the base of its spines, creating a drinking fountain. Butterflies and bees also love the hundreds of tiny purple flowers that grow in a ring around the oval flower head and rise up the cone day by day.

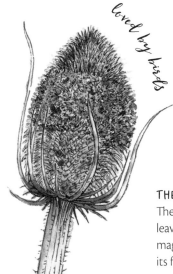

loved by birds

THE MAGIC OF TEASEL
The water collected in its leaves was believed to have magical properties, leading to its folk name 'Venus's basin'.

SOW SEEDS
INDOORS

Uses THE DRIED SEED HEADS OF TEASELS WERE USED AS COMBS TO TEASE OUT KNOTS IN CLOTH IN THE TEXTILE INDUSTRY BEFORE BEING REPLACED BY METAL COMBS IN THE TWENTIETH CENTURY. THEY CAN STILL BE USED TO COMB A PET OR AS A CAT'S SPIKY PLAYTHING.

🧺 AUGUST. HANG SEED HEADS UPSIDE DOWN TO DRY OUT

ERRATIC. POT ON, THEN PLANT OUT BETWEEN AUGUST AND OCTOBER

◆ JANUARY TO APRIL, IN SEED TRAYS, BUT GERMINATION CAN BE

🌷 JULY TO SEPTEMBER

↕🌱 1.5M (4FT 11IN)

49 ▸ MILK THISTLE

₱ *(SILYBUM MARIANUM)*
★ also known as holy thistle, Mary's thistle

Of the different varieties of thistle, milk thistle is the most attractive, with a tuft of purple flowers and milky-white veins running through its large, prickly leaves. Thistles, generally, are thought of as weeds, mostly because they grow where nothing else will. That is a shame as they are nectar-rich and loved by moths, butterflies and bees. Also, their seeds are a nutrient-rich food source for birds.

THE MAGIC OF THISTLES

Stems of the Scotch Thistle were cut, dried and spikes removed to use as walking sticks to keep malicious spirits at bay. The stick was also credited with making men better lovers. The head of a dried thistle can be used as a barometer: when it closes, rain is expected.

OTHER THISTLES

Scotch Thistle (*Onopordum acanthium*): the emblem of Scotland, was introduced into the country in the sixteenth century.
Spear or common thistle (*Cirsium vulgare*): similar to the Scotch thistle, it is classed as a weed and must not be planted in the wild or near agricultural land.
Blessed thistle (*Cnicus benedictus*): an annual plant with a solitary yellow flower. Used in the Middle Ages to treat the bubonic plague and as a tonic, especially for monks. Can be drunk as a tisane to treat colds and indigestion.

loved by butterflies

SEEDS HAVE PARACHUTES

🧺 WHEN THE FLOWER HEADS ARE DRY. SEEDS ARE ATTACHED TO PARACHUTES, LIKE DANDELIONS

ARE TO FLOWER, AFTER THE LAST FROST. SEEDS CAN TAKE 2 WEEKS TO GERMINATE

🔖 AUTUMN OR SPRING, DIRECTLY WHERE THEY

🌱 SUMMER

↕ UP TO 2M (6FT 6IN)

Uses MILK THISTLE CAN BE TAKEN AS A SUPPLEMENT FOR VARIOUS CONDITIONS, SUCH AS INDIGESTION.

WILD STRAWBERRY

🌱 *(FRAGARIA VESCA)*
★ *also known as woodsman's delight*

Appearing like ruby jewels in the summer, wild strawberries have a more intense flavour than their cultivated cousins. Once established, they are also easier to grow, sending out runners with abandon and colonizing large areas of the garden with ease. In fact, to prevent them from taking over your borders, it is wise to contain them in a pot or a window box, where they will provide delicious snacking opportunities within easy reach.

intense flavour

In the wild, they grow at the edges of forests, earning them the folk name woodsman's delight. Folklore suggests that the first strawberry of the season should be given to the birds or the gods of the strawberry patch, although you may not have much choice as birds always find the plumpest ones with ease.

🧺 SUMMER. HARVEST RIPE FRUIT, CUT INTO QUARTERS AND DRY GENTLY IN THE SUN. WHEN THE FLESH IS DRY, THE SEEDS CAN BE RUBBED OFF. STORE IN A COOL, DARK, DRY PLACE

🌱 FEBRUARY, IN SEED TRAYS, COVERING VERY LIGHTLY WITH SOIL (THEY NEED LIGHT TO GERMINATE). MIST TO KEEP MOIST. THE SEEDS TAKE 3 TO 4 WEEKS TO GERMINATE

🌷 MAY (FRUITS: JUNE AND JULY)

↕🌱 5 TO 20CM (2 TO 8IN)

Uses THE SWEET LITTLE BERRIES ARE LOVELY AS A FLAVOURSOME AND DECORATIVE ADDITION TO SUMMER FRUIT SALADS OR SIMPLY POPPED INTO THE MOUTH FOR A NUTRITIOUS ALTERNATIVE TO SWEETS (THEY ARE PACKED WITH VITAMINS B, C AND E). THE LEAVES CAN BE MADE INTO AN INFUSION TO DRINK TO SOOTHE DIGESTIVE PROBLEMS AND TO EASE GOUT AND ARTHRITIS. CRUSH THE BERRIES TO MAKE AN OINTMENT TO CALM SUNBURN.

51 HAWTHORN

🌱 *(CRATAEGUS MONOGYNA)*
★ *also known as hag-thorn, bread and cheese, mayblossom*

A common hedgerow plant in the UK, hawthorn has gnarly, twisted branches and pure white blossom, followed by scarlet berries. It was once thought that witches transformed themselves into hawthorns and it has long been considered unlucky to fell them, so many still stand alone in a field where once they were surrounded by other trees.

scarlet berries

THE MAGIC OF HAWTHORN

There is much folklore surrounding it, mostly relating to its blossom. The tree is in flower on May Day (1 May), the Celtic festival of Beltane, and was part of the celebrations. In Wales, hawthorn crosses were hung over house and stable doors, and branches used to decorate maypoles. It was thought unlucky to bring blossom inside, however: its unpleasant smell (the flowers contain trimethylamine, which occurs in carrion) meant it was linked with death.

Uses A Y-SHAPED BRANCH WOULD MAKE AN EXCELLENT DIVINING ROD. THE FRESH YOUNG LEAVES CAN BE EATEN, HENCE ITS COMMON NAME OF BREAD AND CHEESE. TRADITIONALLY, STRIPS OF CLOTH, KNOWN AS 'CLOOTS', ARE TIED TO TREES NEAR WELLS AND SPRINGS (HENCE THEY ARE CALLED 'CLOOTIE WELLS') IN THE HOPE OF HEALING OR ANSWERS TO PRAYERS.

🧺 LATE SUMMER, WHEN THE HAWS (FRUIT) ARE STILL GREEN. SOAK IN WARM WATER FOR SEVERAL DAYS TO SOFTEN THE FLESH, THEN SQUASH IN A SIEVE TO EXTRACT THE SEEDS

◆ SPRING, IN A SEED TRAY (THEY MAY NOT GERMINATE THE FIRST YEAR BUT PERSIST, THEY MAY IN THE SECOND)

🌱 MAY

🌱 UP TO 15M (50FT) WHEN MATURE

52 ELDER

jewel-like berries

🌱 *(SAMBUCUS NIGRA)*
★ *also known as pipe tree, bur tree, black elder*

An elder tree is small but bountiful, with frothy, scented blossom in summer and dark, jewel-like berries in autumn. It also has furrowed bark and hollow branches, which have a very unpleasant smell. Its seeds are often dispersed by blackbirds, which like to eat the fruit. Seedlings then pop up everywhere and, once established, grow vigorously.

THE MAGIC OF ELDER

Christians in the early Church aligned elder with the workings of the Devil, calling it the 'tree of death'. This may have its origins in legends that Judas hung himself from an elder and that Christ's cross was made from elder wood. This could have been to quash older beliefs that it was a sacred tree. Folklore often relates to countering the Devil, witches and malevolent spirits. Dropping elder pith (from inside a branch) into oil floating in a glass of water, for example, is said to reveal all the local witches. Bathing your eyes in green juice from the wood was also thought to help you see them. In Scotland, if you stood beneath an elder tree on Samhain, then you could see fairies riding past. Modern pagans and druids still regard its blossoms as feminine and a representation of the Mother Goddess.

🧺 PICK THE BERRIES, THEN MASH AND SIEVE TO SEPARATE THE SEEDS FROM THE PULP

◆ TRICKY TO GERMINATE, THEY NEED A PERIOD OF COLD. STORE THE SEEDS IN MOIST PAPER TOWEL IN A BAG IN THE FRIDGE FOR 3 TO 4 MONTHS, THEN GROW IN POTS, SHELTERED, FOR A YEAR BEFORE PLANTING OUT

🌼 MAY UNTIL AUGUST

↕🌱 UP TO 15M (50FT)

Uses AT ONE TIME, CHILDREN USED THE DRIED, HOLLOW YOUNGER BRANCHES TO MAKE PEA-SHOOTERS AND PENNY WHISTLES. THE FLOWERS CAN BE MADE INTO A CORDIAL OR REFRESHING TISANE, THE BERRIES INTO A SYRUP OR WINE. TO MAKE AN ASTRINGENT SKIN TONIC, ADD 25G (ONE OUNCE) OF FLOWERS TO 575ML (2½ CUPS) BOILING WATER. COOL AND STORE IN A SCREW-TOP BOTTLE.

53 WILD BERGAMOT

seed head

P (MONARDA DIDYMA)
★ *also known as bee balm, crimson bee balm, eau-de-cologne plant*

This pretty North American flower grows in the wild along the banks of streams and in ditches, but is equally at home in a garden. Wild bergamot was recognized by Indigenous American people as a useful medicinal plant – it is, in fact, a natural antiseptic – and they used it as a poultice to treat minor wounds and excessive flatulence.

It is a valuable addition to your borders. Its flowers, with their curling tubular petals clustered in whorls, are very pretty and bees can't resist them.

citrussy

SEEDS

Rub the leaves between your finger and thumb and you can see why it is called wild bergamot: the leaves smell citrussy, like the bergamot orange. The whole plant smells lovely – so much so, it has been known to attract hummingbirds.

The seeds are easy to collect once plants have flowered. Simply make sure that the birds have had their feast first, then remove the seed heads and follow the instructions on page 14. Plant somewhere a bit shady with rich, moist soil and it will thrive. Wild bergamot is a herbaceous perennial so will die down but return the following year.

Uses
DRIED BERGAMOT LEAVES MAY BE MADE INTO A HERBAL TEA. AS WELL AS BEING A REFRESHING DRINK, IT MAY ALSO TREAT COLDS AND CONGESTION. THE FLOWERS ARE SAFE TO EAT, TOO, AND MAKE A SUMMER SALAD LOOK VERY PRETTY INDEED.

🧺 SEPTEMBER

🌷 SUMMER

◆ SPRING, DIRECTLY WHERE THEY ARE TO FLOWER, IN A SUNNY SPOT IN RICH, MOIST SOIL

🌱 IM (3FT 3IN)

54 CHICORY

P (CHICORIUM INTYBUS)
★ *also known as succory, blue sailor, Italian dandelion*

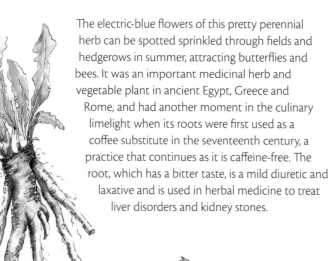

The electric-blue flowers of this pretty perennial herb can be spotted sprinkled through fields and hedgerows in summer, attracting butterflies and bees. It was an important medicinal herb and vegetable plant in ancient Egypt, Greece and Rome, and had another moment in the culinary limelight when its roots were first used as a coffee substitute in the seventeenth century, a practice that continues as it is caffeine-free. The root, which has a bitter taste, is a mild diuretic and laxative and is used in herbal medicine to treat liver disorders and kidney stones.

SEEDS

Uses THE LEAVES AND FLOWERS MAKE A DAINTY ADDITION TO SUMMER SALADS.

THE MAGIC OF CHICORY
Chicory is said to open doors on 25 July if you cut it with a golden knife then hold the cut plant against the keyhole. Do this in silence, otherwise you might die.

🧺 OCTOBER

🌱 JUNE TO SEPTEMBER

◆ MAY, DIRECTLY WHERE THEY ARE TO FLOWER, IN A SUNNY SPOT

↕ 1.2M (3FT 11IN)

A BOWL OF SCENTED LOVELINESS: POTPOURRI

Prolong the sweet scents of summer flowers and aromatic herbs and seeds with this easy make.

Potpourri – a collection of sweet-smelling materials in a bowl – went out of favour when too many were left to gather dust and lost their fragrance. If you keep an eye (and a nose) on one, however, you will be rewarded with a gorgeously scented home at any time of year.

To make, a potpourri, you will need to gather together a mixture of flower petals, leaves and buds, plus a selection of aromatic herbs, seeds and spices. Carefully dry the petals and leaves (see page 64 for how do this) to preserve their colour and scent, so they remain fragrant for as long as possible. There are no hard-and-fast rules about what to include in your bowl of potpourri – it's fun to experiment with different flowers and spices and develop your own fragrance.

Potpourri pointers

★ Try these strongly fragranced plants: rose petals; leaves of sage, bay, lemon balm, bergamot, peppermint, myrtle, rosemary, lemon verbena; flowers of violet, lily of the valley, lavender, chamomile, pinks.

* Include whole flowers and buds to fill out your mixture, such as larkspur and marigold. They are also colourful and look decorative.

* Add crushed or ground spices to liven it up, such as coriander, nutmeg, cloves, cinnamon, allspice, mace, vanilla pods.

* Add a fixative to your mixture. This blends the fragrances and halts evaporation of the essential oils, which are the sources of the scents. Try orris root (from rhizomes of *Iris* 'Florentina') orgum benzoin (from a tree), both available online. Each has its own fragrance so choose which goes best with your mix. Use 1tbsp of fixative to about 1.2 (5 cups) litres of potpourri.

* Pile into a pretty container. To make the fragrance last longer, put a lid on it when the room is empty.

A BEGINNER'S POTPOURRI: LEMONY FRAGRANCE

WHAT YOU NEED

Rose petals
Lemon verbena leaves
Lemon thyme leaves
Lavender flowers
Grated zest of 1 orange
Grated zest of 1 lemon
15g (½oz) allspice
15g (½oz) cloves
50g (2oz) fixative

WHAT YOU DO

Mix 4 parts rose petals to 1 part each of lemon verbena, lemon thyme and lavender flowers. Mix in the orange and lemon zest. Leave for two days, then add spices and fixative. Add 50g (2oz) fixative to 9 litres (2 gallons) of mix. Stir every day for a week then put into your chosen container and inhale deeply. Store in a jar or plastic food storage box with lid for two days before ready to use.

55 CHICKWEED

℗ *(STELLARIA MEDIA)*
★ *also known as white bird's eye, mischievous Jack, adder's mouth*

Most gardeners pull up chickweed rather than treasure it, which is not surprising as it is tremendously invasive and vigorous. There can soon be a blanket of it through your flower beds. This is thanks to the large numbers of seeds it generates – one plant can produce 1,300, four or five times a year – that germinate quickly.

It may look harmless, with its low growth and star-shaped white flowers, but it has managed world domination, cropping up in most countries. The Japanese regard it as a lucky herb and include it in the Festival of Nanakusa-no-sekku, where it is honoured alongside six other herbs on 7 January.

THE MAGIC OF CHICKWEED
It can be carried or used in spells to attract a lover or maintain a friendship.

Uses ADD THE SOFT TOPS TO A SALAD OR MAKE A TEA, WHICH WILL SOOTHE STOMACH INFLAMMATION AND CRAMPS, COUGHS AND SORE THROATS. AN INFUSION OF A SMALL HANDFUL OF ROOTS MAKES A GOOD FACE WASH FOR WINTER-WEARY SKIN.

PLANTS GENERATE
LARGE NUMBERS
OF SEEDS

DOES AN EXCELLENT JOB OF SEED DISPERSAL SO, INSTEAD, KEEP AN EYE ON IT ONCE PLANTED, STOPPING IT FROM SPREADING TOO WIDELY

SELF-SEEDS YEAR ROUND

JUNE TO AUGUST

UP TO 35CM (13³/₄IN)

hooked burr

56 ⟩ BURDOCK

🌱 *(ARCTIUM LAPPA)*
★ also known as beggar's buttons, burrseed, cockleburr, happy major

This stately and handsome biennial plant can be found growing along country lanes and on waste ground. It will also add a regal height to any border and sports deep maroon flowers from July to September, which turn into burrs (seed pods) covered with tiny hooks that cling to clothing and animals' fur. This enables the seeds to be transported, to grow somewhere new.

THE MAGIC OF BURDOCK
Burdock is used for protection – probably because of the bristly appearance of its burrs and the hairiness of its stems – is added to incense and used in spells. In Turkish Anatolia, it was believed to ward off the evil eye and a symbol representing it was woven into kilims. Wise women in medieval times collected it during a waning moon, dried it, cut it into small pieces, then strung it like beads on a red thread to wear to keep safe.

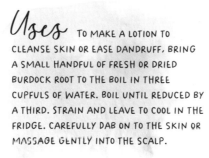

Uses TO MAKE A LOTION TO CLEANSE SKIN OR EASE DANDRUFF, BRING A SMALL HANDFUL OF FRESH OR DRIED BURDOCK ROOT TO THE BOIL IN THREE CUPFULS OF WATER. BOIL UNTIL REDUCED BY A THIRD. STRAIN AND LEAVE TO COOL IN THE FRIDGE. CAREFULLY DAB ON TO THE SKIN OR MASSAGE GENTLY INTO THE SCALP.

FOLK MEDICINE
A bag of burdock seeds hung around the neck was believed to protect the wearer from rheumatism. The whole plant has a variety of healing purposes. A tea made from the root is considered a blood purifier, while a decoction of the root is a remedy for mild stomach ailments. Poultices made from fresh burdock leaves boiled in salted water can be used to soothe bruises and aching limbs.

🧺 AT THE END OF THE SECOND YEAR OF GROWTH

🌾 SEEDS NEED A PERIOD OF COLD TO GERMINATE. SCATTER ON TO PAPER TOWEL, PUT IN A PLASTIC BAG, REFRIGERATE FOR A FEW WEEKS.

THEN SOW DIRECTLY WHERE THEY ARE TO FLOWER, AFTER THE LAST FROSTS

🌱 JULY TO SEPTEMBER

↕🌱 UP TO 2.7M (8FT 10IN)

57 MUGWORT

Ỿ (ARTEMISIA VULGARIS)
★ also known as mother of all herbs, naughty man, sailor's tobacco, St John's plant, traveller's herb

It's hard to ignore mugwort: it is a very tall, statuesque plant with spikes bearing clusters of small yellow flowers along their length. It's known in Germany as the mother of all herbs because of its height and because it has long been used in both herbal medicine (to treat gynaecological problems and as a diuretic) and as a magical plant. It produces huge quantities of seeds, so is good to forage for. Generally regarded as a weed, find it along road verges and patches of neglected grassland (it thrives in undisturbed soil). Pick the entire flower stem and hang it upside down in a bag to collect the seeds as it dries out.

THE MAGIC OF MUGWORT

Folklore has it that putting the leaves in your shoes will maintain your stamina during a long run. To increase its effectiveness, pick it at sunrise while saying the Latin phrase '*Tollam te artemisia, ne lassus sim in via*' ('I will pick you Artemisia, so I will not tire on my way'). It is one of what the Anglo-Saxons called 'St John's herbs' (the others are betony, chamomile, chervil, crab apple, fennel, nettle, plantain and watercress), which are gathered at midsummer for protection against bad luck and evil. Like many herbs, it is at its most powerful when harvested at the summer solstice or a full moon. One of its common names, 'naughty man', comes from its reputation as an aphrodisiac.

SOW SEEDS IN SPRING OR AUTUMN

🧺 OCTOBER

🔶 SPRING OR AUTUMN, PREPARING THE SEEDS AS DESCRIBED FOR MOTHERWORT, AS THESE ALSO NEED COLD TO GERMINATE, THEN SOW

DIRECTLY WHERE THEY ARE TO FLOWER, ALLOWING PLENTY OF SPACE

🌱 JULY TO SEPTEMBER

🌿 UP TO 2M (6FT 7IN)

Uses MUGWORT IS SAID TO BE GOOD AT DETERRING MOTHS. TRY HANGING A BUNCH OF DRIED STEMS IN YOUR WARDROBE. IT IS ALSO USED TO MAKE A NATURAL YELLOW DYE.

58 ▷ MEADOWSWEET

P (FILIPENDULA ULMARIA, SYNONYM: SPIRAEA ULMARIA)
★ *also known as bridewort, trumpet weed, steeplebush*

seed pods

Hedgerows and ditches froth with the white plumes of meadowsweet all summer long, the flowers borne on tall, elegant stems swaying above the less graceful plants below. It's not only lovely however – as John Gerard, a seventeenth-century English herbalist, wrote, 'it makes the heart merrie and joyful and delighteth the senses' – meadowsweet is useful too. It contains salicylic acid, an aspirin-like compound that has pain-relieving and anti-inflammatory properties. A tea made from its flowers was a common remedy for flu and headaches before the advent of aspirin. Meadowsweet has a heavy, sweet scent and tastes like a cross between elderflower and marzipan, so was used to flavour mead (a drink made from fermented honey), which is how it got its name.

Uses INFUSE
A FEW FLOWERS IN HOT MILK OR CREAM – THEIR ALMONDY FLAVOUR MAKE FOR TASTY CUSTARD, RICE PUDDING AND PANNA COTTA.

THE MAGIC OF MEADOWSWEET
Witches use it in love mixtures and in sachets. It was strewn on the floor at weddings, earning it its common name 'bridewort'.

🧺 LATE SUMMER

◆ AUTUMN OR SPRING, DIRECTLY IN RICH, MOIST SOIL IN FULL SUN

🌱 JUNE TO SEPTEMBER

↕ 90 TO 100CM (2FT 11IN TO 3FT 3IN)

59 TANSY

P ◯ *(TANACETUM VULGARE)*
★ *also known as bitter buttons, traveller's rest*

The button-like mustard-coloured flowers of tansy grow in clusters in hedgerows, riverside meadows and on waste ground. They will also happily populate a garden, self-seeding merrily to surprise you. Toxic and bitter, nonetheless, it was a Passover herb – one of the bitter herbs eaten by those who had just ended their Lenten fast. A drink made from its leaves was said to 'expel the worms that have grown lean with hunger'. It was an ingredient of an unpleasant-sounding pudding eaten by Christians in Lent: tansy was combined with wild strawberry leaves, cinquefoil and milk, reduced to a creamy thickness.

toxic and bitter

SOW IN
SEED TRAYS

Uses DO NOT INGEST AS IT IS TOXIC, BUT TANSY FLOWERS ARE GOOD DRIED AS THEY RETAIN THEIR COLOUR AND SHAPE. THEY CAN ALSO BE USED TO MAKE A YELLOW DYE BY SIMMERING THEM IN WATER FOR AN HOUR, THEN STRAINING. DUE TO ITS TOXICITY, TANSY HAS A HISTORY OF BEING USED AS AN INSECT REPELLENT AND WAS STREWN ON FLOORS TO DETER LICE AND FLIES.

THE MAGIC OF TANSY

The plant was sacred to the Greek god Ganymede, who was given it to drink by Zeus to make him immortal. Consequently, it is associated with immortality and eternal youth, so used in spells relating to longevity.

 LATE SUMMER, WHEN
FLOWERS ARE DRY
AND BROWN

GERMINATION CAN BE
ERRATIC

 SPRING OR AUTUMN,
IN SEED TRAYS, BUT

❀ JULY TO SEPTEMBER

⇂❀ UP TO 90CM (2FT 11IN)

60 DANDELION

(TARAXACUM OFFICINALE)
★ also known as fairy clock, hare's lettuce

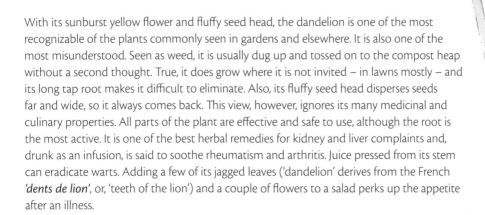

With its sunburst yellow flower and fluffy seed head, the dandelion is one of the most recognizable of the plants commonly seen in gardens and elsewhere. It is also one of the most misunderstood. Seen as weed, it is usually dug up and tossed on to the compost heap without a second thought. True, it does grow where it is not invited – in lawns mostly – and its long tap root makes it difficult to eliminate. Also, its fluffy seed head disperses seeds far and wide, so it always comes back. This view, however, ignores its many medicinal and culinary properties. All parts of the plant are effective and safe to use, although the root is the most active. It is one of the best herbal remedies for kidney and liver complaints and, drunk as an infusion, is said to soothe rheumatism and arthritis. Juice pressed from its stem can eradicate warts. Adding a few of its jagged leaves ('dandelion' derives from the French *'dents de lion'*, or, 'teeth of the lion') and a couple of flowers to a salad perks up the appetite after an illness.

THE MAGIC OF DANDELIONS

Fairies were thought to release the seeds from dandelion clocks by blowing on them. A dandelion buried in the northwestern corner of a house will bring favourable winds.

SEEDS ARE DISPERSED
FAR AND WIDE

Uses SCRUB THE ROOT, DRY IN A VERY LOW OVEN, THEN GRIND WHEN COOL TO MAKE A COFFEE SUBSTITUTE. ADDING WARM MILK AND HONEY IMPROVES THIS GREATLY. TO MAKE A SKIN TONIC, INFUSE ONE TSP OF DRIED DANDELION FLOWERS IN A CUP OF WATER. LEAVE FOR HALF AN HOUR THEN DECANT INTO A BOTTLE WITH A SCREW TOP.

 NO NEED. ONCE YOU HAVE DANDELIONS, YOU WILL ALWAYS HAVE DANDELIONS

SELF-SEEDS YEAR ROUND

 MAY TO JUNE

FLOWERS CAN GROW UP TO 60CM (2FT)

61 ⊳ HENBANE

🌱 ⏺ *(HYOSCYAMUS NIGER)*
★ *also known as stinking Roger, black nightshade, henbells, Devil's eye*

Although not as potent as hemlock, henbane is another fetid, toxic plant that, if ingested, provokes unpleasant illness, including convulsions that can last days and delirious hallucinations accompanied by dilated pupils. It is a shame as it has attractive, funnel-shaped yellow flowers with deep purple centres. Its leaves are big and hairy, though, so that's a give-away.

seeds emit smoke

Uses
HENBANE HAS BEEN USED MEDICALLY TO TREAT RHEUMATISM, TOOTHACHE, COUGHS AND STOMACH ACHE. ITS SEEDS SOMETIMES APPEAR IN INCENSE, BEER AND TEA. ALL OF WHICH IS DONE UNDER CAREFUL REGULATION, HOWEVER, SO IT IS DEFINITELY NOT RECOMMENDED TO TRY THIS AT HOME.

THE MAGIC OF HENBANE
When burnt, henbane seeds emit a smoke that can cause hallucinations and death. Witches were said to do this to induce a state of clairvoyance and gathered the seeds at midsummer to use for ointments and spells. Legend has it that henbane is most potent when gathered naked, standing on the right foot only, using your little finger to the pull the plant from the ground. Quite a palaver when the result could be nausea, vomiting, convulsions and death.

62 ◁ HEMLOCK

🌱 ☠ *(CONIUM MACULATUM)*

★ *also known as herb bennet, poison parsley, kex, musquash root*

With its feathery leaves and pretty white flowers that grow in umbrella-like clusters resembling cow parsley, hemlock looks harmless. It grows vigorously in damp places, like ditches and riverbanks, reaching heights of 2.4m and is anchored sturdily into the ground with a long tap root.

Do not be fooled by its innocent appearance: all parts of this plant are deadly poisonous, but especially the root and the seeds when they are almost ripe.

To recognize it, look for dark purple spots on its hollow stems and leaves, which appear before the plant dies. Be careful: it looks a lot like wild carrot (*Daucus carota*), which also has purple spots, but, unlike that plant, hemlock has hairless stems. Be sure, when you are foraging, not to collect seeds from this plant and definitely do not grow it.

seed head

THE MAGIC OF HEMLOCK

Its fatal qualities and general characteristics – it has a fetid smell, grows in damp places and its leaves and stems are speckled purple as it dies – have led to it being associated with the Devil and the dark arts. Even a small amount of the plant is fatal, as Socrates found out when he was given it to drink when his death sentence was passed in 399BC. This is a plant that it's best to avoid.

SMOKING BUNDLES

Many plants emit an aromatic smoke when allowed to smoulder. Smoking bundles have long been used to cleanse a space during rituals, to heal and to bless.

WHAT YOU DO

Gather a handful of herbs (see the box below for some ideas) and cut them into lengths of around 10cm (4in). You can also use dried flowers (see page 64) to add another layer of scent and prettiness. Tie the stems first with twine, then the entire bundle. Leave until completely dry.

If lighting indoors, open doors and windows first. Light the bundle over the kitchen sink to reduce risk, allowing it to catch fire. After around 20 seconds, blow the flames out and then waft the smoke around the space or person. To extinguish, stub out the bundle in a fireproof bowl.

NOTIONS: MAGICAL MAKES

Some ways to harness the magical properties of seeds and dried flowers.

AROMATIC PLANTS TO GROW AND BURN

Juniper (*Juniperus communis*): said to boost psychic powers.

Lavender (*Lavandula*): invites friendly spirits in; its smoke will cleanse a sacred space.

Mugwort (*Artemisia vulgaris*): is a 'messenger plant', so the smoke from its dried leaves is said to help us connect with nature and to encourage lucid dreaming.

Rosemary (*Salvia rosmarinus*): emits cleansing and purifying smoke that helps with energy flow, strengthens the memory, and protects the space.

Vervain (*Verbena officinalis*): dispels unrequited love. It also brings balance, inner strength and peace.

White sage (*Salvia apiana*): used to disperse negativity, cleanse and heal.

INCENSE CONES

Making your own incense is a cost-effective way to introduce aromatic smoke to magical work or to scent your home, especially if you use dried herbs grown in your garden.

WHAT YOU NEED

3 to 4tbsp mixed dried and powdered herbs and flowers (thoroughly pulverized in a mortar and pestle, or blitzed in a food processor)
1tsp marsh mallow root powder (to hold the mixture together, available online).
1tsp water

WHAT YOU DO

Mix all the powders together in a small bowl. Gradually add the water, drop by drop, and stir to combine until the mixture forms a solid mass. Shape into tall cones and allow to dry. This may take several days, so be patient. When ready, light the tip and allow to burn.

Plants to try: lavender, sage, rosemary, rose, juniper, catmint, hyssop, peppermint, seeds from pine cones.

Magic sachets

Use one with a spell to increase its potency.

WHAT YOU NEED
Herbs, seeds and spices appropriate to your intention, fresh or dried
A handkerchief-size piece of material
Favourite crystal (optional)
Thread, string or ribbon in a colour appropriate to your intention.

WHAT YOU DO
Place the herbs, seeds and spices in the centre of the material. Add the crystal, if using. Gather the four corners of the material and tie firmly with the thread string or ribbon. Hang above a door or bed depending on the spell.

IDEAS FOR SACHET CONTENTS AND COLOURS
For love: pink with apple, basil, dill, jasmine, lavender, thyme, rose, sage.

For abundance: green with comfrey, honeysuckle.

For protection: blue with bay, fennel.

For health: blue with acorns, rue, rosehips.

For fertility: green with mustard, poppy.

63 COMFREY

P (SYMPHYTUM OFFICINALE)
★ *also known as gooseberry pie, suckers, church bells, pigweed*

Comfrey is difficult to miss – this tall perennial plant can grow up to 90cm (2ft 11in) and has big, rough leaves. Look for it in damp places, such as waste ground and field boundaries. Comfrey is a first-class composting plant, as it helps to break down the other materials, and is good as a mulch around other plants in the growing season. Alternatively, it can be made it into comfrey tea, which is a natural fertilizer. To make, heap young leaves into a bucket, fill with water, cover with a lid and leave. After a few weeks, dilute with water to use as a liquid feed for your garden plants.

THE MAGIC OF COMFREY
Comfrey had a reputation for mending bones – hence its less common names of 'boneset' and 'knitbone'. Wet leaves were applied over small fractures like a vegetable plaster. Probably not recommended these days.

— SEEDS

Uses TO MAKE A SOOTHING FACE PACK, PUT 4TBSP BOILING WATER INTO A BLENDER WITH A HANDFUL OF CHOPPED COMFREY LEAVES. BLEND UNTIL SMOOTH. STRAIN THROUGH A PIECE OF MUSLIN INTO A JUG, PRESSING TO EXTRACT AS MUCH LIQUID AS POSSIBLE. SMOOTH ON TO CLEAN SKIN AND LEAVE FOR 10 MINUTES. THEN, WASH OFF WITH WARM WATER, PAT DRY AND APPLY MOISTURIZER.

🧺 OCTOBER

🌷 JULY TO SEPTEMBER

◆ EARLY SPRING, DIRECTLY WHERE THEY ARE TO FLOWER

↕🌱 60 TO 90CM (2FT TO 2FT 11IN)

64 ◀ NETTLE

🌱 *(URTICA DIOICA)*
★ *also known as hokey-pokey, sting-leaf, Devil's apron*

The stinging and invasive nature of the nettle means that it is usually seen as something to banish from the garden, but it has many beneficial qualities and uses. While it is a good idea to keep it in check, it is also wise to save some, as the nettle is highly nutritious – rich in antioxidants, protein, calcium, iron, magnesium and vitamins A, B, C and D. The young tips and leaves can be steamed and eaten like spinach, made into a nourishing soup or drunk as a tea. The plant is also used to soothe skin and digestive problems, treat arthritis and gout, ease headaches and anaemia, even staunch nosebleeds and soothe dog bites. Nettle seeds, too, are mineral-rich, boosting the health of skin and hair.

Uses

BOILING FRESH NETTLE LEAVES PRODUCES A VIBRANT GREEN DYE. THE ROOTS PRODUCE A WARM YELLOW DYE IF BOILED WITH ALUM. A NETTLE TISANE (SEE PAGE 112) IS A REMEDY FOR RHEUMATISM. A CUP IN THE MORNING, AT LUNCH AND SUPPER IS SAID TO WORK LIKE MAGIC. TO GAIN BENEFIT FROM THE SEEDS, SPRINKLE ON SALADS, IN SANDWICHES OR BLEND INTO SMOOTHIES.

SIEVE SEEDS
TO SEPARATE

THE MAGIC OF NETTLES

If you are the subject of a curse, nettles can lift it and put it on the person who initiated it. Throwing nettles on to a fire keeps danger away. Holding nettles in your hand will ward off ghosts. Wearing nettle roots as an amulet will keep negativity away. Seven strips of nettles tied into seven knots can be used as a charm to ward off ill fortune. Seven strips woven into the mane of a horse or tail of cattle will protect them from harm and illness.

🧺 EARLY SEPTEMBER, WEARING GLOVES, CUT WHOLE STEMS. HANG THEM UPSIDE DOWN TO DRY WITH TOPS IN A BAG, THEN SIEVE TO SEPARATE THE SEEDS. WILL ALSO SELF-SEED READILY

◆ SPRING, DIRECTLY WHERE THEY ARE TO FLOWER

🌱 MAY TO SEPTEMBER, BUT DOES NOT FLOWER IN FIRST YEAR

↧🌱 UP TO 1.2M (3FT 11IN)

65 ◀ LARKSPUR

🌱 ⚫ *(CONSOLIDA REGALIS, SYNONYM: DELPHINIUM CONSOLIDA)*
★ *also known as lark's heel, knight's spur, staggerweed*

Tall with bright blue flowers, larkspur towers regally over humbler flowers in summer borders. Larkspur (**Consolida**) is an annual, but is a cousin of the perennial delphiniums. The Latin name, '*Delphinium*', comes from a Greek word, '*delphinion*', as the unfolding flower resembles a dolphin's head. The heads open into five-petalled flowers along the length of the long stems. Growing from seed is easy and rewarding, plus they self-seed, so will reappear the following summer.

THE MAGIC OF LARKSPUR
According to *Cunningham's Encyclopedia of Magical Herbs*, larkspur keeps away ghosts, and the flowers frighten off scorpions and other venomous creatures. Looking into a midsummer fire through a bunch of larkspur was said to give you trouble-free vision until the following midsummer.

SOW SEEDS DIRECTLY IN LATE SUMMER OR AUTUMN

Uses ALL PARTS OF LARKSPUR ARE POISONOUS IN LARGE DOSES, BUT ESPECIALLY THE SEEDS, SO USE WITH CAUTION AND DON'T TAKE INTERNALLY. THE JUICE OF THE PETALS, HOWEVER, MIXED WITH A LITTLE ALUM (AVAILABLE FROM CHEMISTS AND ONLINE), MAKES A GOOD BLUE INK.

🧺 AUGUST, BUT SELF-SEEDS READILY

🌷 JUNE TO AUGUST

🌱 UP TO 1M (3FT 3IN)

🔖 SEPTEMBER OR SPRING IN SEED TRAYS OR MODULES

66 ❯ YEW

🌱 ⓘ *(TAXUS BACCATA)*
★ *also known as tree of death*

Evergreen and ancient, the yew is easily recognizable from its needle-like leaves, scarlet berries and deeply ridged, reddish-brown bark. Its dense green-black foliage, its ability to live to a great age (2,000 years in some cases), its poisonous leaves and seeds, and its prevalence in graveyards, have given it a macabre reputation.

red, fleshy berries

THE MAGIC OF THE YEW
The yew's ability to renew itself (by branches dropping down and growing into new trunks) symbolizes immortality and regeneration. In Ireland it is one of the five sacred Guardian Trees brought back from the otherworld by a tall stranger (along with oak, ash, apple and hazel). Superstition says to avoid it during a storm, as it is likely that witches will be sheltering there. Branches from the tree were also used to light Beltane bonfires, and twigs of yew were thrown on to the coffins of the dead, to help them on their way.

MIX SEEDS WITH SAND TO SPEED UP GERMINATION

🧺 AUTUMN, WEARING GLOVES, MASH RIPE BERRIES TO FREE SEEDS, THEN PUT IN A SIEVE AND RINSE TO CLEAN

🪨 SEEDS CAN TAKE 2 YEARS TO GERMINATE. TO SPEED THEM UP, WEARING GLOVES, MIX THE SEEDS WITH SHARP SAND AND

KEEP IN WARM, MOIST CONDITIONS AT AROUND 21°C FOR 4 TO 5 MONTHS. THEN, IN SPRING, SOW DIRECTLY WHERE THEY ARE TO GROW

🌺 MARCH AND APRIL

↕🌱 12M (40FT) OR MORE, BUT OFTEN PRUNED AS HEDGES

Uses BE AWARE THAT YEW FOLIAGE IS HIGHLY POISONOUS SO MUST NOT BE USED FOR ANY REMEDIES OR BEAUTY PREPARATIONS. THE SEED INSIDE THE RED FLESHY BERRY IS EXTREMELY TOXIC. HANDLE WITH CARE, PREFERABLY WITH GLOVES. BRANCHES MAKE GOOD WANDS, THOUGH.

 # 67 ▶ MONKSHOOD

FINGER-LIKE SEED PODS

🌱 ⓘ *(ACONITUM NAPELLUS)*
★ *also known as wolfsbane, aconite, Thor's hat, old wives' hat*

This attractive plant, with its deep purple flowers borne on tall, graceful stems, is also deadly. Every part of it is poisonous, although the root is the most toxic of all, causing stomach ache, giddiness, heart problems, even death. Avoid ingesting it, however, and you have a lovely flowering plant that lasts well as a cut flower. Its flowers resemble a hood (hence its many common names) and its finger-like seed pods look as though they have claws.

Monkshood features in many stories and legends. Greek myth credits it as being a plant of Hades, king of the underworld, that it sprung from the spittle of his three-headed dog, Cerberus. It is also associated with Hecate, Greek goddess of magic, witchcraft and the night. In Hinduism, it is sacred to Shiva, who saved the world by drinking poison. He turned blue and spilt a few drops of the poison on the ground. Those drops became monkshood.

THE MAGIC OF MONKSHOOD
Folkore has it that it was added to sachets to guard against vampires and werewolves. Wrapping the seed in lizard's skin and carrying it in your pocket might enable you to become invisible at will.

Uses DO NOT CONSUME – ENJOY AS A CUT FLOWER INSTEAD.

🧺 SEPTEMBER

◆ SEPTEMBER, TO PLANT OUT THE FOLLOWING YEAR. SEEDS NEED TO BE EXPOSED TO COLD TO GERMINATE. GERMINATION CAN TAKE AS LONG AS 2 YEARS

🌷 FROM JUNE TO AUGUST

↨🌱 UP TO IM (3FT 3IN)

GREAT MULLEIN

(VERBASCUM THAPSUS)

★ also known as Jupiter's staff, blanket herb, hare's beard

Mullein reaches for the sky, growing an impressive spire of tiny yellow flowers up to 2m (6ft 6in) tall, surrounded lower down by huge, grey, velvety leaves, its long tap root securing it firmly into the ground. Each flower opens before sunrise and closes by mid afternoon. The flowers mature from the bottom to the top of the spike in spirals., then turn into capsules of tiny seeds, which are carried on the wind, landing and germinating in places that humans have forgotten – around industrial parks, beside fences, in car parks. It will also grow well in a garden, of course, but does need a lot of space to be shown off at its best.

THE MAGIC OF MULLEIN

Folklore has it that flowers placed beneath your pillow prevent nightmares. In India, the plant is used to guard against evil spirits.

SEEDS CAN
BE STORED

Uses THE DOWNY STEMS OF MULLEIN CAN BE USED AS WICKS IN CANDLES AND OIL LAMPS. YOU CAN ALSO INFUSE THE FLOWERS IN WATER TO SOOTHE SORE FEET.

🧺 AS SOON AS THE FRUITS (SEED PODS) APPEAR. THERE CAN BE UP TO 300 SEED PODS PER PLANT, EACH CONTAINING BETWEEN 500 AND 800 TINY SEEDS. THE SEEDS LAST WELL AND CAN BE STORED FOR YEARS

🏷️ SPRING, IN SEED TRAYS, BUT SELF-SEEDS READILY

🌷 JUNE TO SEPTEMBER

↕🌱 1 TO 2M (3FT 3IN TO 6FT 6IN)

69 ▷ MAGNOLIA

🌱 (MAGNOLIA GRANDIFLORA)

★ also known as blue magnolia, star magnolia

ripe seeds in the pod

The beautiful, tulip-shaped blooms of magnolia open on bare branches at various times of the year depending on the species (there are over 200). Magnolia stellata flowers as winter ends and the gorgeous flowers seen against a blue sky are a sure sign that warmer days are ahead. Magnolia grandiflora opens in late summer, giving the garden a touch of glamour at the season's end.

THE MAGIC OF MAGNOLIA

Placing a few magnolia flowers under the bed is supposed to maintain a faithful relationship. In Japan, lingering under a magnolia tree is discouraged as its heady scent is said to stun or even kill (this is not true!). Japanese brides often include magnolia flowers in their bouquets as a symbol of the purity of their love.

Uses IF YOU ARE GOOD AT WHITTLING, MAGNOLIA WOOD CAN BE USED TO MAKE A DOWSING ROD. THE BARK IS USED IN TRADITIONAL CHINESE MEDICINE TO TACKLE ANXIETY AND INSOMNIA.

NOTE: BEFORE COLLECTING SEEDS, FIND OUT IF THE TREE IS A HYBRID. IF IT IS, THE SEEDS WON'T BREED TRUE (PLANTS MAY NOT RESEMBLE THE PARENT), WHICH WILL TAKE 10 TO 15 YEARS TO DISCOVER, WHEN THE TREE WILL FIRST FLOWER

🧺 STRAIGHT FROM THE POD, WHEN BERRIES ARE BRIGHT RED AND RIPE. IMMEDIATELY REMOVE THE BERRY FLESH AND SOAK THE SEEDS IN LUKEWARM WATER OVERNIGHT. NEXT DAY, RUB SEEDS WITH A ROUGH CLOTH TO REMOVE THEIR OUTER COATING. PUT IN A CONTAINER OF MOIST SAND AND MIX WELL, THEN STORE IN THE FRIDGE, UNDISTURBED, FOR AT LEAST 3 MONTHS

🌾 SPRING, EITHER IN POTS OR DIRECTLY WHERE THEY ARE TO FLOWER

🌷 SPRING

↕🌿 RANGES FROM A SMALL SHRUB TO A LARGE TREE, DEPENDING ON SPECIES

◂ # MARIGOLD

℗ (CALENDULA OFFICINALIS)
★ *also known as bride of the sun, summer's bride, ruddles*

Marigolds' cheery bright orange or yellow flowers track the sun throughout the day. Originating from India, that may be why they are used to decorate Hindu altars and made into decorative garlands, representing the sun and symbolizing positive energy.

THE MAGIC OF MARIGOLDS

In Wales, if the flower did not open before 7am, it meant there would be thunder that day. In Devon and Wiltshire, though, to pick marigolds meant thunder would follow. According to *Cunningham's Encyclopedia of Magical Herbs*, if a girl touches the petals with her bare feet, she will understand the language of the birds.

harvest seeds when dry

🧺 WHEN FLOWER HEADS ARE FULLY BROWN AND DRY

🌱 EARLY SPRING, THEN IN SUCCESSION, EVERY 2 TO 3 WEEKS, TO EXTEND FLOWERING TIME. SOW DIRECTLY WHERE THEY ARE TO FLOWER

🌷 JUNE TO SEPTEMBER

↕🌱 UP TO 40CM (1FT 3IN)

Uses MARIGOLD FLOWERS ARE FREQUENTLY USED IN FOLK MEDICINE AND COSMETICS. THEY HAVE SOOTHING AND SOFTENING QUALITIES WHEN BLENDED INTO AN OINTMENT, FOR EXAMPLE, WHICH IS EXCELLENT FOR SUNBURN. TEA MADE FROM THE FLOWERS IS WORTH A TRY (SWEETEN WITH HONEY IF NECESSARY). SCATTERING THE PETALS ON SALADS PROVIDES A DECORATIVE SPLASH OF COLOUR. THEY ARE ALSO A GOOD COMPANION PLANT IN VEG BEDS AS THEY ATTRACT APHID-EATING HOVERFLIES.

Decoctions: the method used to extract the active ingredients of roots, stems and seeds.

DECOCTIONS

WHAT YOU DO

Place the root, stem or seeds in a saucepan and cover with water. Bring to the boil and simmer for 10 to 15 minutes. Set aside to cool. Sieve out the solids, then use the liquid.

POTIONS: FOLK MEDICINE

Herbs used for medicinal purposes can be prepared in different ways to ensure that they are administered effectively. These potions are all easy to make in your own kitchen and need few ingredients.

Tinctures: like decoctions but made with alcohol, so they can be stored for longer.

TINCTURES

WHAT YOU DO

Pulverize 2tbsp fresh herbs in mortar and pestle or blitz in a food processor. Mix with 250ml (1 cup) alcohol (rubbing alcohol, available from pharmacies, or vodka). Store in a screw-top jar in a warm place for three to four weeks, shaking jar daily. Strain through muslin and store in a clean screw-top jar. Dilute with water as required.

Poultices: soothing patches of herbyness to apply to aching muscles and sore areas.

WHAT YOU DO

Crush a handful of fresh herbs in a mortar and pestle or food processor. Spread the resulting pulp on a piece of muslin, fold in half and place between two plates over a pan of boiling water. Apply to the afflicted area as hot as is bearable.

OINTMENTS

Ointments: a thick balm to apply to sore or sunburnt skin.

WHAT YOU DO

Crush 25g (1oz) herbs in a mortar and pestle or food processor. Slowly heat 112g (4oz) petroleum jelly in a pan. When it has melted, add the herbs, then stir until boiling. Simmer gently for 20 minutes. Strain into small pots and lay greaseproof paper circles on top when cold.

Syrups: used to treat sore throats and colds.

WHAT YOU DO

Pour 300ml (1¼ cups) of boiling water on to 75g (2½oz) crushed herbs or seeds. Leave to cool, then strain liquid into a small pan. Heat until warm, then add 112g (4oz) sugar. When it has melted, bring mixture to the boil and simmer gently until syrupy. Cool slightly, then put in a bottle with a stopper.

71 ◁ HELLEBORE

🌿 ⓘ *(HELLEBORUS)*
★ also known as Christmas rose, Lenten rose

Rarely seen in the wild, hellebores are perennial garden plants that brighten gardens when all else is dormant in winter and early spring. Their demure but beautiful flowers thrive in the shade and their leaves retain their glossiness all year.

THE MAGIC OF HELLEBORES

Green hellebore (*Helleborus viridis*) was once thought to be used by sorcerers to irritate opponents, thought how this was achieved remains vague. It was also thought that if you scattered hellebore flowers before you, you would become invisible.

Uses HELLEBORES ARE POISONOUS SO ARE NOT USED IN ANY REMEDIES OR TEAS.

GATHER SEEDS IN SUMMER

🧺 PROPAGATE BY DIVISION (GROWING FROM SEED IS DIFFICULT) IN EARLY AUTUMN OR SPRING. AFTER FLOWERING, DIVIDE PLANTS AND PLANT STRAIGHT AWAY

🌷 JANUARY TO FEBRUARY

🌱 UP TO 45CM (1FT 6IN)

72 ▷ SCARLET PIMPERNEL

℗ ◐ (ANAGALLIS ARVENSIS)
★ also known as blessed herb, shepherd's clock, John-go-to-bed-at-noon

petals close in the rain

Found sprawling on waste ground and sand dunes, this annual plant brightens forgotten places with its bright orange to red (sometimes blue and pink) flowers. One of the most charming, and useful, things about it is that the flowers open around 7am and close again at 2pm (thus earning it its the folk name of John-go-to-bed-at-noon). The petals also close as rain approaches.

The flower, famously, is the symbol of the Scarlet Pimpernel, the alias of protagonist Sir Percy Blakeney in the novel of the same name by Baroness Emmuska Orczy.

THE MAGIC OF SCARLET PIMPERNEL

Witches cleanse their athame (magical knife) with the juice of scarlet pimpernel to empower them. It is supposed to give the gift of second sight to anyone who holds it.

UPPER PART OF THE SEED CAPSULE OPENS, RELEASING RIPE SEEDS

🧺 WHEN THE SEED CAPSULES ARE DRY, BEFORE THE WIND DISPERSES THEM. THERE ARE 35 TO 40 SEEDS PER CAPSULE

◆ APRIL, DIRECTLY WHERE THEY ARE TO FLOWER

🌱 JUNE TO SEPTEMBER

↕🌱 UP TO 30CM (12IN)

Uses THE PLANT IS TOXIC SO DO NOT CONSUME.

73 ▷ DAISY

℗ *(BELLIS PERENNIS)*
★ *also known as bruisewort, moon daisy, field daisy*

The simple, open flower of a daisy makes it one of the most loved of the wild flowers. There are more than 4,000 species, but the one found in lawns is the one we usually think of. It is often associated with innocence and children. It is also a symbol of summer, as anyone who has lain in a field and made a daisy chain or pulled off its petals muttering 'he loves me, he loves me not' knows. Indeed, it is said that summer hasn't arrived until you can tread on 12 daisies with one foot. The name 'daisy' comes from the Anglo-Saxon *'daeges eage'*, which means 'days' eye'. This reflects how its petals open in the morning and close in the evening.

he loves me, he loves me not

SOW IN A SEED TRAY

Uses DAISIES LOOK PRETTY ADDED TO HERBAL TEA. TEA MADE SOLELY USING DAISIES IS SAID TO COMBAT COLDS AND COUGHS. USED IN A POULTICE, THEY REDUCE BRUISING (HENCE ITS COMMON NAME OF 'BRUISEWORT'.)

THE MAGIC OF DAISIES
Sleep with a daisy root under your pillow and an absent lover may return to you. A daisy chain placed around a child's neck is said to offer protection from being kidnapped by fairies (it will also look very cute).

🧺 SEPTEMBER TO OCTOBER, WHEN COMPLETELY DRY

🌑 LATE SUMMER OR EARLY AUTUMN IN A SEED TRAY

🌱 APRIL TO OCTOBER

 ↕🌱 UP TO 15CM (6IN)

74 HEARTSEASE

🌱 *(VIOLA TRICOLOR)*
★ *also known as wild pansy, love-in-idleness*

This dainty little plant, with its small, pansy-like blooms, has the most enchanting name, which derives from its association with love and 'easing of the heart'. It flowers from early spring until autumn, with plenty of opportunities to look for it in fields, meadows or coastal dunes. It is also easy to grow a pot or two from seed.

The whole plant, including its roots, is used in remedies to soothe and relieve migraine and to calm skin conditions.

SHAKE THE
SEEDS OUT

THE MAGIC OF HEARTSEASE
This demure little plant is believed to be especially potent if used in love charms and spells. In *A Midsummer Night's Dream*, fairy king Oberon instructs Puck to fetch a herb that will make Queen Titania fall in love with the first creature she sees. He picks heartsease.

Uses A CLOTH DIPPED INTO AN INFUSION OF HEARTSEASE THEN WRAPPED AROUND A PAINFUL JOINT FOR 15 MINUTES CAN PROVIDE SOME COMFORT AND RELIEF.

🧺 IN SUMMER WHEN THE SEED PODS ARE A PALE STRAW COLOUR. THE SEEDS SHOULD BE A LIGHT BROWN, NOT WHITE (IF WHITE, THEY'RE NOT RIPE). THEY ARE TINY, SO PUT THE POD INTO A CONTAINER BEFORE SHAKING THE SEEDS OUT

◆ MARCH AND APRIL UNDER COVER, THEN PLANT OUT IN SPRING

🌱 EARLY SUMMER TO EARLY AUTUMN

↕🌱 ABOUT 20CM (8IN)

75 ⟩ JOE PYE WEED

🌱 (*EUTROCHIUM FISTULOSUM, SYNONYMS: EUPATORIUM FISTULOSUM, EUPATORIADELPHUS FISTULOSUS*)

★ *also known as trumpet weed, queen of the meadow*

Flowering in late summer, this North American wild flower brings a welcome fresh flush of pinky-purple flowers on tall stems when all else is fading. Butterflies love it. It is named after the Christianized version of a name taken by a Mohican chief originally called Schauquethequeat, who lived in Massachusetts from 1740 to 1785.

THE MAGIC OF JOE PYE WEED

Popping a few leaves into your pocket was said to earn you the respect of everyone you encountered, while putting them under your tongue would guarantee success in romance.

STORE SEEDS IN
THE FRIDGE

Uses A TEA CAN BE MADE FROM THE ROOTS, LEAVES OR DRIED FLOWERS. GATHER THE LEAVES IN SUMMER, BEFORE THE FLOWER BUDS OPEN, AND HARVEST THE ROOTS IN THE AUTUMN. IT WAS USED BY INDIGENOUS AMERICANS TO TREAT FEVERS AND KIDNEY STONES.

🧺 LATE SEPTEMBER

 AUTUMN: STORE SEEDS FOR 4 WEEKS BEFORE PLANTING
SPRING: STORE IN THE FRIDGE IN AN OPEN PAPER BAG FOR AT LEAST 6 WEEKS BEFORE PLANTING, TO HELP THEM GERMINATE

🌷 SEPTEMBER

⬇🌱 UP TO 2M (6FT 6IN)

76 ⟨ COWSLIP

P *(PRIMULA VERIS)*
★ *also known as peagles, buckles, fairy cup, herb Peter, plumrocks*

This sweetly scented wild flower was once widespread in British pastures and meadows but is now less so. All the more reason to cultivate it yourself! It grows very well in gardens and naturalizes happily, creating a gorgeous flush of nodding yellow, bell-shaped flowers in spring.

Uses
TRY AN INFUSION OF THE FLOWERS (WHICH ARE THE EFFECTIVE PART OF THE PLANT) TO EASE RESPIRATORY INFECTIONS. THEY ALSO LOOK LOVELY AS CAKE DECORATIONS AND CAN BE MADE INTO WINE.

THE MAGIC OF COWSLIPS
Placing a flower under the door mat is said to discourage unwanted visitors. More generously, holding a bunch of flowers will help you find hidden treasure.

🧺 AUGUST TO SEPTEMBER, WHEN SEEDS ARE RIPE

🌷 APRIL TO MAY

↕🌱 5 TO 20CM (2 TO 8IN)

◈ AS SOON AS POSSIBLE AFTER COLLECTING, IN LIGHT SHADE ON ANY WELL-DRAINED SOIL OR IN SEED TRAYS

TISANES: HEALTHY, HAPPY DRINKS

Tisanes are what most of us think of as herbal teas: drinks made from infusions of plants, herbs and spices in hot water. (Tea is only made from the *Camellia sinensis* plant, from which tea leaves are harvested.) Whatever they are called ('herbal infusions' is another name), there are endless variations of these drinks, they are quick and easy to prepare and could do you a whole heap of good.

How to make a tisane

WHAT YOU NEED

Plant or plants of your choice: herbs, flowers, leaves, seeds and spices, fruit and bark all have a place in a tisane. Try different combinations – the options are countless.

You can make a tisane in a cup, mug or ordinary teapot, or you could invest in a glass teapot known as a *'tisanière'*. It has a central perforated tube to put the herbs, seeds and so on in. When the tisane has infused sufficiently, this is removed, straining the drink.

WHAT YOU DO

Crush any leafy material in your hands to release the essential oils. Place in the teapot (or cup). Pour water that hasn't quite boiled over it. Cover with the lid (or place saucer over cup), to prevent the oils evaporating in the steam. Leave for 5 minutes or so (this varies depending on taste and ingredients), strain and drink.

CLASSIC TISANES

Lemon verbena, lemon balm: a useful pick-me-up when spirits are flagging.

Peppermint: good for digestion, indigestion and colds.

Rosemary: an invigorating stimulant.

Fennel seed: freshens the breath.

WINNING COMBINATIONS

★ Lemon balm, mint, lavender.

★ Rosemary, orange peel, cloves, honey.

★ Lemon rind and rosemary.

★ Lavender and orange.

VARIETIES

★ Leaf tisanes: such as lemon verbena, mint, lemon balm, rosemary sage.

 ★ Bark tisanes: such as cinnamon, slippery elm, black cherry.

★ Fruit tisanes: such as raspberry or blackcurrant leaves, fruit pieces, lemon and orange peel.

 ★ Flower tisanes: such as rosehips, lavender, chamomile, dandelion, clover.

★ Seed tisanes: such as cardamon, fennel, caraway, coriander.

TWO ICED TISANES

Make as you would a hot tisane, but leave to cool and serve in ice-filled glasses.

★ Lemon balm and lavender leaves.

★ Nettle leaves and sprigs of rosemary.

77 ⟨ LESSER PERIWINKLE

🌱 ⬤ *(VINCA MINOR)*
★ *also known as sorcerer's violet, Dicky Dilver, cut finger, blue buttons*

This herbaceous perennial is a common sight in many gardens. It's popular because it flourishes in shade – always a tricky spot to plant – and covers the ground with trailing stems, mauve or white five-petalled flowers and glossy leaves.

Its familiarity, however, belies its many, sometimes dark, folkloric associations. In Italy, it was called the '*fiore di morte*' (flower of death) because it was often included in children's funeral wreaths (purple being the colour of mourning). In England, men were garlanded with it on their way to the gallows, and, in Wales, if you picked it from a grave, you would be haunted by the dead person lying below.

THE MAGIC OF THE LESSER PERIWINKLE

Despite these macabre associations, periwinkle was also seen as a means of protection against bad luck. It was worn around the neck to keep misfortune at bay, and farmers put bunches of it over animal shelters to keep livestock safe. It was also said to make people fall, and stay, in love.

In his *Complete Herbal*, Culpeper suggests that 'Periwinkle leaves eaten by man and wif together to cause love – which is rare quality indeed if true.' In his sixteenth-century *The Book of Secretes*, Albertus Magus, similarly, suggests that periwinkles, sempervivums and worms of the earth be ground to a powder and served on meals to men and women to arouse love, but it seems unlikely and a great deal of trouble.

SEEDS ARE
SLOW TO GROW

Uses VINCA MINOR AND VINCA MAJOR ARE MILDLY TOXIC, SO DO NOT TO USE FOR SELF-MEDICATION OR IN AN INFUSION.

🧺 PERIWINKLE IS VERY SLOW TO GROW FROM SEED. IT'S BEST TO BUY A PLANT INSTEAD OR PROPOGATE BY DIVISION OR CUTTINGS

🌷 MARCH AND APRIL

 10CM (4IN)

edible berries

78 MYRTLE

℗ (MYRTUS COMMUNIS)
★ also known as bride's myrtle, Roman myrtle, sweet myrtle

love herb

This thoroughly delightful plant looks good all year round. It has glossy, evergreen leaves, an abundance of white flowers with numerous fibre-optic-like stamens in summer, followed by round purple berries containing several seeds in autumn. It can be clipped into interesting shapes and grows away happily in a pot.

Perhaps it's because of its generous disposition that myrtle has long been considered a 'love herb'. In ancient Greece, it was associated with Venus, who wore a garland of myrtle leaves around her head. Myrtle certainly thrives if grown with love and pride, and a healthy plant is said to be an indication of a good gardener.

COLLECT SEEDS IN SEPTEMBER

ROYAL MYRTLE
All royal brides in the UK have a sprig of myrtle in their bouquet, a tradition started by Queen Victoria when she married Prince Albert. On their wedding day in 1840, a little myrtle bush was planted on the east façade of Fulham Palace. A cutting taken from that bush was later grown and planted at Osborne House, their home on the Isle of Wight. When Victoria's daughter, also called Victoria, got married, she incorporated a sprig from that plant in her bouquet, and so it has continued ever since.

Uses THE FLOWERS AND FRUIT OF MYRTLE ARE BOTH EDIBLE. THE BERRIES CAN BE EATEN FRESH WHEN RIPE, MADE INTO A DRINK OR DRIED TO USE AS AN AROMATIC FLAVOURING IN MIDDLE-EASTERN DISHES. AN ESSENTIAL OIL CAN BE MADE FROM THE LEAVES AND BRANCHES.

🧺 SEPTEMBER

🌷 JULY AND AUGUST

◆ AUTUMN, IN A COLD FRAME, TRANSPLANTING OUTDOORS IN SPRING

⥥🌱 UP TO 3.5M (1½IN)

79 ⟩ LAVENDER

fragrant

℗ (LAVANDULA ANGUSTIFOLIA)
★ *also known as elf leaf, nard, spike*

It's impossible to walk past a lavender bush without plucking a flower head to hold under the nose and sniff. This woody, shrubby plant with narrow, silver leaves and purple spikes of flowers is native to the Mediterranean but has made its home around the world. Its name comes from the Roman word *'lavare'*, which means 'to wash', as its flowers have been made into oil to fragrance perfumes and other cosmetics for centuries.

HARVEST SEEDS
WHEN THE
FLOWERS ARE DRY

THE MAGIC OF LAVENDER

Perhaps it's the heady scent that makes lavender a natural to use in love potions and sachets: who can resist its intoxicating fragrance? Lavender was also scattered on floors to bring peace to the home and release a fresh scent when walked on. Placing it under a pillow while thinking of a wish was a way to make it come true. Dreaming of the wish meant that it had been granted.

 WHEN THE FLOWERS ARE COMPLETELY DRY. TEST BY SHAKING: IF SEEDS FALL OUT, THEY'RE READY

FEBRUARY TO JULY, ON SURFACE IN SEED TRAYS

JULY TO AUGUST

 30 TO 90CM (1FT TO 2FT 11IN)

Uses THERE ARE COUNTLESS WAYS, IN COSMETICS, COOKING AND FOLK MEDICINE. THE SCENT AIDS PEACEFUL SLEEP. SIMILARLY, ADDING LAVENDER FLOWER HEADS OR OIL TO A BATH MAKES FOR A CALMING, FRAGRANT SOAK. A FEW FLOWER HEADS INFUSED IN HOT WATER AND DRUNK IN SMALL QUANTITIES IS SAID TO RELIEVE FATIGUE AND PERK YOU UP. A LITTLE LAVENDER OIL APPLIED TO THE TEMPLES CAN EASE HEADACHES. ITS STRONG FLAVOUR IS LESS POPULAR IN COOKING, BUT LAVENDER SUGAR IS DELICIOUS. CHOP A FEW FLOWER HEADS IN A FOOD PROCESSOR, ADD SUGAR AND BLITZ – PERFECT ON SHORTBREAD OR STRAWBERRIES.

80 ⟩ HONESTY

P *(LUNARIA ANNUA)*
★ *also known as pennywort, money flower, moonwort, silver plate, grandmother's spectacles.*

The silvery, disc-shaped seed pods of honesty rise above flower beds in late summer like tiny full moons. This has not escaped notice: its Latin name is '*Lunaria*' and some of its common ones include the word 'moon'. In the USA, though, it's called 'silver dollar', also for obvious reasons. The fact that the paper-thin, translucent seed heads reveal their contents so blatantly likely inspired its most common name, 'honesty'.

Before the seed heads appear, clusters of purple flowers are carried on tall, upright stems, adding height and drama to the garden. There are several varieties of honesty to choose from, including hardy annuals and biennials, plus another perennial variety. All are easy to grow and very rewarding.

brings good luck

THE MAGIC OF HONESTY
Legend has it that honesty only thrives where the gardener is of good character. Witchcraft credits it with the power to open locks, recover lost property and to bring good luck and wealth to those carrying a sprig in their pocket.

Uses BRING THE LUNAR MAGIC OF HONESTY INDOORS BY COLLECTING THE SEED HEADS AND DRYING THEM. THEY LOOK GRE ON THEIR OWN IN A VASE OR COMBINED WITH OTHER DRIED PLANTS AND FLOWERS.

🧺 TOWARDS THE END OF SUMMER, WHEN THE SEED HEADS CRACKLE TO THE TOUCH, BUT IT WILL SELF-SEED READILY IF YOU LET IT

📦 EARLY SUMMER, WHERE THEY ARE TO FLOWER, WHICH THEY WILL DO THE FOLLOWING SPRING

🌷 LATE SPRING, EARLY SUMMER

↕🌱 UP TO IM (3FT 3IN)

81 ⟨ NASTURTIUM

(TROPAEOLUM MAJUS)
★ *also known as Indian cress, cress of Peru, lark's heel*

The colourful, glamorous flowers of the nasturtium are a clue to its origins. It is a native of South America, brought to Spain and then Europe by the conquistadors in the sixteenth century. It is now a common sight, trailing from pots or scrambling through late summer borders. The trumpet-shaped flowers have a prominent spur at the back and are held above lily-pad-shaped leaves. The seeds are easy to spot, as they are large and wrinkled, like mini brains, and often grow in clusters of three. Like the rest of the plant, they have a spicy flavour, which is how it got it its name: 'nasturtium' is a derivative of the Latin **'nasus tortus'**, which means twisted nose.

SPICY
FLAVOUR

Nasturtiums are often sown as a companion plant as they are said to repel various bugs and beetles from crops such as squash, broccoli and cucumber. An extract is also used as a spray on fruit trees to keep aphids away.

THE MAGIC OF NASTURTIUMS
Dried leaves can be added to an incense mix used to cleanse the home. Nasturtiums are also said to have aphrodisiac properties.

🧺 LATE SUMMER OR EARLY AUTUMN — THEY SHOULD BE BEIGE, DRY AND FALL OFF THE PLANT EASILY

🌷 MAY TO OCTOBER

🌱 UP TO 20CM (8IN), DEPENDING ON VARIETY

MID MAY, DIRECTLY WHERE THEY ARE TO FLOWER, IN A SUNNY SPOT, IN POOR SOIL

Uses FLOWER BUDS AND SEEDS, PRESERVED IN VINEGAR, ARE USED AS A SUBSTITUTE FOR CAPERS IN PASTA SAUCES, ON PIZZAS AND SO ON. USE THE FLOWERS AND LEAVES TO ADD SUNSHINE COLOURS AND A SHARP, MUSTARDY FLAVOUR TO SUMMER SALADS. THE FLOWERS CAN ALSO BE STUFFED WITH GUACAMOLE OR CREAM CHEESE FOR A TASTY STARTER OR SIDE DISH.

82 ‹ SNAPDRAGON

P (ANTIRRHINUM MAJUS)
★ *also known as calf's snout, dragon's mouth*

As any child knows, if you squeeze the throat of a snapdragon, its 'jaws' open and snap shut, just like a dragon – hence its common name. A common sight in hanging baskets and window boxes, this perennial plant is mostly grown as an ornamental.

THE MAGIC OF SNAPDRAGONS
Eat the skull-like seeds and it is said that you will regain lost beauty. If you are walking outside and feeling that evil is approaching, step on a snapdragon and, poof, the evil will vanish. Also, wearing a necklace of its seeds is said to ensure that you will never become bewitched.

Uses AN INFUSION OF SNAPDRAGON LEAVES IS USED TO PURIFY THE LIVER. A POULTICE OF LEAVES CAN SOOTHE MINOR BURNS. SOME EXPONENTS OF NATURAL DYEING EXTRACT A GREEN DYE FROM ITS FLOWERS.

USE FRESH SEEDS FOR QUALITY PLANTS

seed pods resemble skulls

🧺 COLLECTING SEEDS IS EASY, BUT MAY RESULT IN POOR PLANTS. FOR BEST RESULTS, BUY FRESH SEEDS

🌷 JULY TO OCTOBER

↧🌱 UP TO 2M (6½FT)

◆ AUTUMN, IN SEED TRAYS, OVERWINTERING IN A COLD FRAME, OR SPRING, DIRECTLY WHERE THEY ARE TO FLOWER, IN FULL SUN

83 CORNFLOWER

♃ *(CENTAUREA CYANUS)*
★ *also known as batchelor's button, bluebottle*

This annual wild flower bursts vigorously out of the ground in early spring, its bright blue flowers on long silver-grey stems attracting bees and butterflies in great numbers. Previously regarded as a weed in cornfields, it is now a rarer sight than it was as herbicides have driven it out. It is easy to grow in the garden and will spread itself around, springing up in surprising places and bringing with it a shot of electric blue. It is also a good plant for the cutting garden, as it is easy to grow and lasts well in a vase.

THE MAGIC OF CORNFLOWERS

A bag of dried cornflowers hung by the front door is believed to ward off bad energy. They are also used in fertility and abundance spells and to communicate with the fairy world.

SEEDS ARE LARGE
AND EASY TO HANDLE

Uses THE DRIED FLOWERS LOOK PRETTY IN A BOWL OF POTPOURRI OR CAN BE INFUSED IN HOT WATER TO CREATE A DELICATELY COLOURED TEA. IF YOUR EYES ARE TIRED, ADD SOME FLOWERS TO HOT WATER, COOL AND THEN USE AS AN EYEWASH.

🧺 SEPTEMBER — LOOK FOR THE PALE, STRAW-LIKE SEED HEADS

🌷 JUNE TO SEPTEMBER

↕🌱 FROM 90CM TO 1.5M (2FT 11IN TO 4FT 11IN), DEPENDING ON WHEN THEY WERE SOWN (AUTUMN-SOWN PLANTS ARE BIGGER)

🌱 SOW THE LARGE SEEDS AS SOON AS YOU HAVE COLLECTED THEM (SEPTEMBER OR, IF IT'S MILD, UP TO OCTOBER)

84 ► AMARANTH

P (AMARANTHUS CAUDATUS)
★ *also known as love-lies-bleeding, tassel flower*

A striking plant that grows up to 2.5m (8ft 2in) and has dangling tassels of crimson flowers, amaranth is easy to grow from seed. It brings a dash of colour and flamboyance to flower beds in late summer and early autumn.

Most parts of this plant are edible, including its leaves and seeds. Some species of amaranth are cultivated as a food crop in India and South America: its many seeds (grain) are ground to make flour.

SEEDS CAN BE GROUND TO MAKE FLOUR

THE MAGIC OF AMARANTH

A spell using the dried flowers is said to help mend a broken heart or make an unwanted admirer back off (amaranth is credited with cooling passion and ardour). In the Victorian language of flowers, however, amaranth – called by its common name of love-lies-bleeding – stood for hopeless love.

 LATE SUMMER AND AUTUMN

🌷 JULY TO AUGUST

 MID TO LATE SPRING, DIRECTLY WHERE THEY ARE TO FLOWER, IN A SUNNY SPOT

↕🌱 60CM (2FT)

Uses WEAR A CROWN OF AMARANTH ON ASCENSION DAY IF YOU WISH TO BECOME INVISIBLE (ALTHOUGH IT WILL PROBABLY DRAW MORE ATTENTION RATHER THAN HELP YOU TO DISAPPEAR).

FACE MASK*

WHAT YOU NEED

1 or 2 handfuls of herb(s) of your choice (see box this page), yoghurt or oats

In a small bowl, pour half a cup of boiling water over the herb(s). Infuse for 15 minutes, strain and cool. Mix in some yoghurt or oats to make a paste and leave for 30 minutes. Cleanse face thoroughly, spread mask over, avoiding eyes and mouth. Lie down and relax for 15 minutes. Wash off with warm water, then splash with cold water and pat dry.

LOTIONS: PLANT BEAUTY

A few herbs and flowers combined with kitchen cupboard ingredients can be whipped up, at little cost, into beauty treatments that won't harm you or the planet.

FACE MASK HERBS TO SUIT YOUR SKIN TYPE

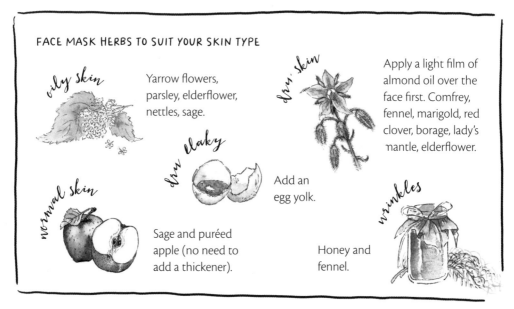

oily skin
Yarrow flowers, parsley, elderflower, nettles, sage.

dry skin
Apply a light film of almond oil over the face first. Comfrey, fennel, marigold, red clover, borage, lady's mantle, elderflower.

dry flaky
Add an egg yolk.

normal skin
Sage and puréed apple (no need to add a thickener).

wrinkles
Honey and fennel.

* **Remember:** check sell-by date on the yoghurt; do a patch test first on the side of your neck to see how your skin will react; use the mask on the day you make it.

MARIGOLD FLOWER WATER

WHAT YOU NEED

50g (2oz) marigold petals, 800ml (3¼ cups) water

Simmer half the petals gently in the water for 30 minutes. Strain the liquid into a clean pan, discarding the petals, and repeat, adding the remaining fresh petals. Cool and strain into sterilized jars. Leave for three days before using.

ROSE WATER

WHAT YOU NEED

50g (2oz) rose petals (wild dog rose or sweetbriar rose are best), water

Put half the petals in a pan with enough water to cover. Bring to the boil, simmer for 30 minutes, then strain the liquid into a clean pan, discarding the petals. Repeat, adding the remaining fresh petals. Cool and strain into sterilized jars. Leave for three days before using.

MOISTURIZER

WHAT YOU NEED

2tbsp glycerine, 2tbsp rose water, 2tbsp marigold flower water

Whisk all the ingredients together. Store in a screw-top bottle. Shake before use, then smooth lightly over the skin.

Reviving soaks

Adding herbs to bath water is a relaxing, healing experience that perfumes the body and the bathroom. It can also soften the skin and correct minor skin disorders.

WHAT YOU NEED
Piece of muslin 20cm (8in) square (ready-made pouches with drawstrings are available online); handful of chopped fresh or dried herbs (see suggested mixtures); string or ribbon, 1tbsp oats (optional, to soften the water)

Place the herbs in the centre of the muslin square (or in the muslin pouch). Gather the corners of the muslin together around the herbs, then tie tightly with the string or ribbon. Dangle beneath the hot water tap as you run the bath so that maximum fragrance and goodness is whooshed into the water. You could also add a decoction of a particular herb (see page 104) to the bath water for a similar effect.

SUGGESTED MIXTURES
Chamomile, lavender and thyme
Yarrow, fennel, sage, rosemary
Lovage, marigold petals
and elderflowers

♀ *(PRUNELLA VULGARIS)*
★ *also known as all-heal, heart of the earth, woundwort, touch and heal*

This low-lying, creeping plant gets its name from its reputation for staunching bleeding. It has been used worldwide to heal wounds, thyroid problems, conjunctivitis and even cancer, although none of the claims have been proven scientifically. In Chinese medicine, it is used to treat dizziness, dry cough, dermatitis and boils.

Selfheal likes short turf and often pops up in lawns, peppering the grass with its spiky purple flowers, often accompanied by white clover in a pretty wild-flower tapestry.

THE MAGIC OF SELFHEAL
Even though it's a common wild flower, there is very little folk magic associated with it, but it has been said that if you pick it, the Devil will come to carry you away.

seed head

SEEDS
GERMINATE
EASILY

Uses FOR A GOOD
MOUTHWASH AND GARGLE FOR A
SORE THROAT, INFUSE IN BOILING
WATER, STEEP FOR 10 MINUTES,
THEN USE WHEN COOL ENOUGH.

🧺 AUGUST TO OCTOBER

🌷 JUNE TO NOVEMBER

◣ SPRING OR AUTUMN, DIRECTLY WHERE THEY ARE TO FLOWER OR IN SEED TRAYS

⇅🌱 20 TO 30CM (8 TO 12IN)

86 › JUNIPER

🌿 (JUNIPERUS COMMUNIS)
★ also known as melmot berries, horse-saver, gin berry

It's all about the fragrance with this evergreen shrub. All parts of the plant emit a lovely aromatic scent, which is released when crushing the spiny leaves or burning the wood. It does flower, producing small yellow blooms, but usually it's grown for its attractive habit, which looks good all year.

aromatic scent

THE MAGIC OF JUNIPER
Considered a deterrent against the Devil and his cohorts, juniper was hung over doors on Beltane Eve (30 April) and burnt at Samhain (31 October) to keep them away. The wood burns with almost invisible smoke, so could be employed stealthily. Also thought of as a guardian of the dead, keeping them safe until ready to be reincarnated, it is sometimes planted on graves.

🧺 SEPTEMBER TO DECEMBER. JUNIPER BERRIES, OR CONES TAKE 2 YEARS TO MATURE — THEY ARE GREEN THE FIRST YEAR, THEN BLUE-BLACK BY THE END OF THE SECOND, WHICH IS WHEN TO PICK THEM

◆ EXTRACTING SEED FROM BERRIES IS DIFFICULT. PERHAPS ONLY TO BE ATTEMPTED IF YOU ARE REALLY DETERMINED. IT'S BEST TO BUY A PLANT INSTEAD

↕🌿 BETWEEN 5M AND 8M (16FT 5IN TO 26FT), DEPENDING ON WHETHER IT'S GROWN AS A TREE OR A SHRUB

Uses
THE FRAGRANT WOOD OF JUNIPER, ESPECIALLY WHEN BURNT, HAS BEEN USED IN FOLK MEDICINE ACROSS EUROPE FOR CENTURIES TO SEE OFF VARIOUS DISEASES. IT IS ALSO SAID TO REPEL INSECTS. THE WOOD IS GOOD FOR CARVING, WOODTURNING AND TO BURN WHEN SMOKING FOOD. WHEN COOKING, ADDING A FEW BERRIES TO THE WATER WHEN BOILING OR STEAMING CABBAGE GIVES IT A TASTY BOOST. THE MOST ILLUSTRIOUS USE OF JUNIPER, HOWEVER, IS IN THE MAKING OF GIN: IT GIVES GIN ITS DISTINCTIVE FLAVOUR!

87 ◁ FORGET-ME-NOT

P (MYOSOTIS SYLVATICA)
★ *also known as mouse ear, scorpion grass*

In spring, earth once bare and unpromising suddenly whooshes into life with a froth of sky-blue or pink flowers. The forget-me-knots have arrived! Once you have grown a single forget-me-not, you will never be without them, as they scatter their seeds all over the place and turn up in surprising and uninvited places. Even so, they are hard not to love. First, they are utterly charming, with tiny, five-petalled flowers with yellow centres growing in clusters. Second, they have the most sentimental name in horticulture (which is probably related to their prolific nature). Their Latin name derives from the Greek words '*mus*' and '*ous*', meaning 'mouse ear', the shape of the plant's tiny petals. Finally, bees can't get enough of them.

THE MAGIC OF FORGET-ME-NOTS
If travelling on the 29 February (that is, a leap day), be sure to wear forget-me-knots in your buttonhole for good luck.

Uses HISTORICALLY, ITS FLOWERS WERE CRUSHED AND APPLIED TO SMALL CUTS TO SLOW DOWN BLEEDING. TODAY, YOU MIGHT PREFER THE FLOWERS ON SALADS.

🧺 END OF MAY, WHEN IT HAS FINISHED FLOWERING

🏷 FROM EARLY SPRING, EITHER IN SEED TRAYS, OR DIRECTLY WHERE THEY ARE TO FLOWER, AFTER LAST FROSTS

🌷 APRIL AND MAY

↨🌱 UP TO 60CM (2FT)

88 FOXGLOVE

℗ 🛈 *(DIGITALIS PURPUREA)*
★ *also known as goblins, witches' thimbles*

By mid summer, foxgloves have sprung up everywhere, their pinkish-purple bell-shaped flower stems spearing woodland glades and poking up among garden shrubs. Folklore has it that if left to self-seed, foxgloves will drive away evil spirits, which is handy as they scatter their seeds liberally.

All is not peachy in the world of foxgloves, however. Thoroughly poisonous, they contain toxins that increase the heart rate and cause nausea, headaches, diarrhoea and kidney problems, so they must not be eaten or used in any remedies. A chemical they contain, however, called digitalis, has been developed into pharmaceutical drugs used to treat heart conditions with a great deal of success.

SCATTERS SEEDS
LIBERALLY

Uses ALL PARTS OF THE FOXGLOVE ARE POISONOUS, SO BE CAREFUL HOW YOU USE IT. THE LONG, STRAIGHT STEMS WERE ONCE USED TO MAKE HANDLES FOR PARASOLS. THE BEST USE FOR THIS CLEVER PLANT, HOWEVER, IS AS A BUFFET FOR BEES, WHICH LOVE IT.

THE MAGIC OF FOXGLOVES

It used to be unlucky to bring foxgloves inside, as they encouraged witches. In Wales, a black dye was made from the leaves to paint crosses on stone floors to banish evil. In Scandinavia, fairies were thought to tell foxes to ring foxglove bells, to warn them of hunters. The name 'foxglove' may come from 'folks glove', as it was said 'fair folk' (fairies) lived in the flowers.

 AUGUST AND SEPTEMBER   🌼 MAY TO JULY, IN SECOND YEAR, AS BIENNIAL

 MARCH AND APRIL, SOW DIRECTLY WHERE THEY ARE TO FLOWER

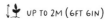 UP TO 2M (6FT 6IN)

89 ST JOHN'S WORT

P *(HYPERICUM PERFORATUM)*

★ *also known as goat weed, amber, rose of Sharon, chase Devil*

SEEDS

There are various explanations given for how the name of this cheery plant with its sunny blooms came to be derived. One is that it was used by the Knights of the Order of St John to heal the wounds they sustained during the crusades. Another that it is associated with John the Baptist, whose 'blood' appears spattered on the flowers on the anniversary of his beheading (29 August). It is also in full bloom around the summer solstice and on St John's Day (24 June), when it is said that its powers are at their height. These powers are both magical and medicinal. It has been used to cure minor ailments and as a painkiller for centuries. Its small, thin leaves have little perforations that can be seen if held up to the light. These are transparent oil glands that contain the same oil as the flower and it is this that is used in remedies. Nowadays, St John's wort is readily available as tablets from pharmacies and taken to lighten depression and calm the nerves.

Uses RUB ST JOHN'S WORT OIL OVER YOUR HANDS IN THE EVENING TO PREVENT AGE SPOTS. A POULTICE OF THE LEAVES (SEE PAGE 105) WILL RELIEVE SKIN IRRITATIONS, BURNS AND BRUISES.

THE MAGIC OF ST JOHN'S WORT

It was said to keep melancholy at bay if gathered at midsummer or on a Friday, with the dew still on it. Generally, it is supposed to banish bad and scary things – like thunder, witches, demons and evil. A vase of flowers in the window will do the trick.

'Wort' is an Anglo-Saxon word meaning 'medicinal' and is attached to many plants, providing a clue to their former use.

🧺 AUTUMN, WHEN SEED PODS ARE COMPLETELY DRY AND BROWN

🌱 JUNE TO AUGUST

🌱 UP TO 1.5M (4FT 11IN)

🔺 MAY, DIRECTLY WHERE THEY ARE TO FLOWER

90 ▸ POPPY

℘ (PAPAVER RHOEAS)
★also known as blind buff, blindeyes, headaches

Tap the seed pod of a poppy and hundreds of tiny blue-grey seeds will tip out into your palm: each plant produces an average of 17,000 seeds. Less than 1mm (about 1/64in) long, in the wild these kidney-shaped seeds are rattled out of the pods by the wind and scattered widely. They then settle beneath the soil before springing into vibrant life in early summer, filling fields and gardens with their beautiful, open, papery blooms. This burst of joyful colour, seemingly from nowhere, has led to poppies being associated with regeneration and rebirth. The spherical seed pods that follow in autumn, with their circular ruffs, on top are equally lovely.

IF THE POD RATTLES, THE SEEDS ARE RIPE

THE MAGIC OF THE POPPY
The poppy is a feminine plant and resonates to the energy of the moon and the element of water. Its seeds can be added to food or a love sachet to attract love. If you have a niggling question that you need to find an answer to, write it on a scrap of paper in blue ink and tuck it into a seed pod. Put the pod beneath your pillow and the answer will be revealed in a dream.

🧺 LATE SUMMER. SHAKE THE SEED POD – IF IT RATTLES, THE SEEDS ARE RIPE (USUALLY 80 TO 90 DAYS AFTER SOWING – ANY EARLIER AND THEY WON'T BE VIABLE)

◆ MARCH TO MAY, DIRECTLY, BUT WILL FLOWER THE FOLLOWING YEAR

🌱 JUNE TO SEPTEMBER

↕🌱 UP TO 60CM (2FT)

Uses POPPY SEEDS ARE OFTEN SPRINKLED OVER BREADS AND PASTRIES. A RICH SOURCE OF MINERALS, MAKE A DELICIOUS, CRUNCHY SALAD BY MIXING ONE TSP SEEDS WITH SIX PEELED AND GRATED CARROTS, THE JUICE OF A SMALL LEMON, FOUR TBSP OLIVE OIL AND ONE TSP CASTER SUGAR.

🌿 ⚠️ *(LONICERA PERICLYMENUM)*
★ also known as woodbine, eglantine

On a summer evening, the scent of honeysuckle can catch you unawares, causing you to stop to inhale its honeyed fragrance deeply. A climbing plant, it scrambles through trees and up trellises happily, sending showers of creamy yellow flowers tinged with purple tumbling down. It is the essence of summer and of a country garden.

Honeysuckle's delicious scent is used in many aromatherapy and cosmetic products, as it is credited with easing skin conditions, improving digestion and calming sunburn, among many other things. The bees and butterflies love it, as do the moths, which sup its nectar during the night. Once pollinated, the flowers change colour slightly. Birds love the berries that follow, but they are toxic if eaten in large quantities, so don't try it.

THE MAGIC OF HONEYSUCKLE

In Scottish folklore, it kept witches, fevers and the ill-intentioned at bay if grown over the front door. If placed around a green candle, it is said to attract money. To heighten psychic powers, try rubbing crushed fresh flowers on your forehead.

EXTRACT SEEDS FROM BERRIES

Uses HONEYSUCKLE SYRUP CAN BE MADE BY PUTTING 150G (5¼OZ) SUGAR, 250ML (1 CUP) WATER AND 50 OR SO FLOWERS IN A SAUCEPAN. BRING TO THE BOIL, REDUCE THE HEAT AND SIMMER FOR AROUND 4 MINUTES. REMOVE FROM HEAT, COOL AND STORE IN A STERILIZED BOTTLE. THE RESULT IS SUMMER IN A BOTTLE! DRIZZLE ON ICE-CREAM, ADD TO YOGHURT OR DILUTED WITH SPARKLING WATER FOR A REFRESHING DRINK.

🧺 WHEN THE BERRIES ARE RED IN AUTUMN

◆ EXTRACT SEEDS FROM BERRIES AND SOW STRAIGHT AWAY IN POTS OF GARDEN SOIL. LEAVE TO GERMINATE IN A COLD FRAME OR IN THE FRIDGE OVER WINTER, THEN BRING BACK OUT IN SPRING (THEY NEED A TEMPERATURE OF 15°C TO GERMINATE)

🌷 SUMMER

↕🌱 DEPENDS ON WHAT IT SCRAMBLES OVER

92 SUNFLOWER

(HELIANTHUS ANNUUS)
★ also known as marigold of Peru

One of the easiest and most rewarding plants to grow from seed, each one producing a gorgeous, gigantic bloom in just a few months. Originally from Peru, these statuesque plants, with stout, hairy stems, were much valued by the Aztecs, who adorned their temples with gold representations of them, their priestesses wearing crowns fashioned from the flowers.

THE MAGIC OF SUNFLOWERS

The golden, disc-shaped flowers track the sun through the day, so many of its magical associations are solar. Its Latin name, '*Helianthus*' refers to Helio, the Titan god of the sun in Greek mythology. Folklore has it that if you cut a sunflower at sunrise and make a wish, it will come true before sunset, so long as the wish isn't extravagant, that is.

nutty taste

Uses WHEN JUST RIPE, THE SEED KERNELS HAVE A NUTTY TASTE THAT IS A FLAVOURSOME ADDITION TO SALADS OR SOUPS. ALSO GOOD IN HOME-MADE GRANOLA OR SIMPLY LIGHTLY ROASTED IN OIL AND DIPPED IN SEA SALT AS NIBBLES. A SYRUP (SEE PAGE 105) MADE WITH THE SEEDS CAN BE USED TO TREAT CHESTY COUGHS. STRIPPED OF LEAVES, THE DRIED, HOLLOW STALKS MAKE GOOD KINDLING.

🧺 SEPTEMBER

❀ JULY, AUGUST

◆ LATE APRIL, DIRECTLY WHERE THEY ARE TO FLOWER, IN A SUNNY SPOT, ALLOWING THEM SPACE

⇕❀ UP TO 3.6M (9³/₄FT)

93 LADY'S MANTLE

℗ *(ALCHEMILLA VULGARIS)*
★ *also known as bear's foot, nine hooks, dew cup*

This generous plant scatters its seeds widely, so having one growing happily means you will be blessed with plenty more. Its yellowy-green flowers fizz into life in early summer, softening the edges of flower beds, paths and lawns. You will also have the joy, after rain or when there is dew, of finding perfect spheres of water nestled on its water-repellant leaves.

THE MAGIC OF LADY'S MANTLE

Those miraculous round drops of water have been attributed with many holy and mystical properties. Alchemists in the Middle Ages, looking to turn base metal into gold, used it in their experiments, albeit with no success. Thus, its Latin name, '*Alchemilla*', derives from the Arab word for 'alchemy', '*alkimiya*'. It was also used to treat many illnesses, including menstrual problems, and was said to restore a woman's beauty. Associated with several goddesses, including Freya, wife of Odin, its common name relates to the Virgin Mary, its curly leaves likened to her cloak, or, 'mantle'.

Uses FILL A SMALL CLOTH BAG WITH DRIED FLOWERS IF YOU SUFFER FROM INSOMNIA. THE FLOWERS CAN ALSO BE USED TO MAKE A NATURAL YELLOW/GREEN DYE.

🧺 OCTOBER, BUT NO NEED, AS SELF-SEEDS READILY

🌱 SPRING, DIRECTLY WHERE THEY ARE TO FLOWER, ALMOST ANYWHERE

🌷 JUNE TO SEPTEMBER

↕🌱 20CM (8IN)

packed with vitamins

❦ *(ROSA)*
★ *also known as wild rose, prickly rose, bristly rose, Arctic rose*

Maybe it's the heart-shaped petals, heavenly scent or sheer abundance of beautiful blooms that have led to the rose being linked with romance for centuries. Roman brides wore a crown of roses, and Cleopatra was said to have seduced Mark Anthony on a bed of rose petals. Today, couples are showered with rose petal confetti after they have said their 'I dos', and petals are strewn over the bed in honeymoon suites in hotels to create a romantic atmosphere.

There are many, many wild and cultivated varieties. The wild dog rose (*Rosa canina*) scrambles through hedgerows, dotting them with pale pink flowers, followed by glossy red hips (the fruit containing its seeds). An essential oil called attar of roses, extracted from the petals of the damask rose (*Rosa x damascene*), is highly prized for use in perfumes and cosmetics.

THE MAGIC OF ROSES

Unsurprisingly, roses appear in many love potions, charms and spells. Rose water (see page 123 for how to make it) added to a bath is said to encourage love, as are rosehips worn as beads (not a hot look, it must be said). Scatter petals throughout the house to maintain calm and equilibrium among family members.

REMOVE SEEDS
FROM HIPS

🧺 AUTUMN, WHEN RIPE, AFTER FIRST LIGHT FROST. SPLIT HIPS IN HALF, REMOVE SEEDS AND RINSE

TO 12 WEEKS BEFORE PLANTING IN SPRING. POT ON SEEDLINGS IN SPRING BEFORE PLANTING OUT

🫙 SEEDS NEED A PERIOD OF COLD STORAGE. PUT IN A PLASTIC BAG IN THE FRIDGE AND KEEP MOIST FOR 10

🌷 MID SUMMER

🌱 DEPENDS ON VARIETY

Uses THE HIPS OF THE WILD DOG ROSE HAVE 20 TIMES MORE VITAMIN C THAN ORANGES, WEIGHT FOR WEIGHT. THUS, A SYRUP MADE FROM THEM PREVENTS COLDS AND SOOTHES SORE THROATS. IT ALSO MAKES A DELICIOUS TOPPING FOR ICE-CREAM AND FLAVOURING FOR YOGHURT.

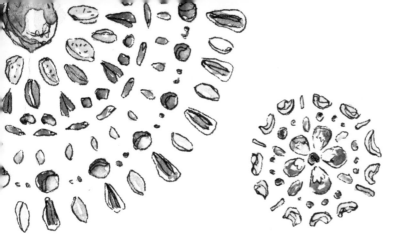

MAKE A SEED MANDALA

Mandalas are circular, geometric arrangements around a central point that are used in meditation and for spiritual guidance in various belief systems. Indeed, 'mandala' is the Sanskrit word for circle. In Tibetan Buddhism, a mandala is a diagram or symbol of an ideal universe, contemplated during meditation. In Hinduism, it is a map representing different deities. Making a mandala from seeds, however, can be a meditative as well as a creative process for everyone.

WHAT YOU NEED

Seeds of different sizes and shapes: spend some time sorting those you have already collected or start collecting seeds to make into a mandala at a later date. You could also use seeds sourced from a shop. Star anise makes a strong centrepiece, for example, and many spices and seeds, like linseed, pumpkin or mung beans, make good fillers. Gather a reasonable quantity of each; the loveliness of a mandala is, in part, due to rhythm and repetition. Arrange them in piles, so you can pick and choose between them easily.

A piece of cardboard to display seeds on: alternatively, you could arrange the seeds on a patch of ground outdoors and let the wind and rain wash the mandala away when it is finished. This taps into the Buddhist concept of impermanence – how nothing is fixed and everything changes. Tibetan Buddhist monks create intricate mandalas from sand, only to destroy them when they are finished.

Glue: to fix the seeds to the cardboard.

A pencil: to sketch the outline of your design before you start.

WHAT YOU DO

Draw a circle, then mark the centre. Draw
an even number of 'spokes' (12 works
well), reaching from the centre out to the
circumference at regular intervals.

Build your mandala from the centre outwards,
starting with a single seed or arrangement in the
middle. Use the 'spokes' as guides to lay your
seeds in ever-increasing rings until they reach
the outer edge.

Work mindfully, giving each seed the respect
it deserves. This is a good time to think about
your personal growth and how to cultivate your
own 'green shoots'. Pay attention to what you
are making and allow yourself to become lost in
the process.

Look at what you have made and let your mind
journey into the centre. Acknowledge any
thoughts that arise and then let them go.

95 ANGELICA

♂ (ANGELICA ARCHANGELICA)
★ also known as wild celery, angel's plant

Reaching a towering height, angelica is easily spotted and identified. Its stem is hollow and furrowed, with large leaves sprouting along its length, and tiny creamy white/greenish flowers are massed around one large, round umbel.

Angelica has long been cultivated for its medicinal properties and perfume (it is sweetly scented), and its leaf stalks are preserved in sugar to use in confectionery (see page 105) or to flavour herbal liqueurs. This is especially true in Scandinavia, where it is used in aquavits. The roots are also used in absinthes. Angelica seeds may also be burned to fill your home with its sweet fragrance.

sweet fragrance

ROOT

THE MAGIC OF ANGELICA

Angelica was once thought to have 'heavenly powers', hence its common name of angel's plant. The etymological root, however, is the Greek word *'angelos'*, which means 'messenger'. An English folklore custom recommends wearing angelica around your neck to protect yourself from evil. Gypsies in Devon are said to hang it over their doors for the same reason.

🧺 SEPTEMBER

🌷 JULY TO AUGUST

◆ DIRECTLY WHERE THEY ARE TO FLOWER. ANGELICA WILL FLOWER IN THE SECOND YEAR OF GROWTH

↧🌱 2M (6FT 6IN)

Uses MAKE A SYRUP WITH THE STEM AND LEAVES OR A DECOCTION OF THE ROOTS AND STORE IN A SCREW-TOP JAR IN THE FRIDGE. DILUTE WITH WATER FOR A REFRESHING DRINK. ADD A MUSLIN BAG OF ANGELICA LEAVES TO THE WATER FOR A RELAXING BATH.

96 YARROW

℗ *(ACHILLEA MILLEFOLIUM)*
★ *also known as nosebleed, sneezewort, Devil's plaything, staunchgrass, old man's pepper*

Yarrow's many common names are an indication of its popularity and that it has long been used. It grows in abundance, its creeping rootstock and very many seeds ensuring supplies are plentiful. Its feathery leaves are topped by a mass of white or pale pink flowers in a flat-topped cluster with a rather spicy scent. A couple of its common names refer to its use as a plug to stop nosebleeds and to staunch bleeding wounds, and its Latin name, '*Achillea*', refers to the myth of Achilles, who used it to heal his wounded soldiers. The plant does contain antibiotic compounds, so there is some truth to this.

THE MAGIC OF YARROW
Fifty dried yarrow stalks are used when consulting the Chinese divination text *I Ching.*

spicy scent

Uses A YARROW INFUSION CAN BE USED TO RINSE HAIR TO HELP CLEAR MILD CASES OF DANDRUFF.

SEEDS

🧺 LATE SUMMER OR EARLY AUTUMN, WHEN FLOWERS ARE BROWN. SEEDS CAN BE STORED FOR UP TO 2 YEARS

◼ SPRING OR AUTUMN, IN SEED TRAYS OR DIRECTLY

WHERE THEY ARE TO FLOWER

🌱 JUNE TO SEPTEMBER

↕🌱 UP TO 75CM (2FT 5IN)

97 ⟨ PRIMROSE

P (PRIMULA VULGARIS)
★ *also known as butter rose*

Primroses are among the first blooms of the year (their Latin name '*Primula*' means 'firstling') and never fail to lift the spirits, punctuating the gloom with their cheery open faces and pale yellow flowers. Growing in clusters like ready-made bouquets, the flowers appear before the leaves, each with five, notched petals that are darker at the centre. They are also loved by butterflies and other pollinators and often grow in areas of ancient woodland. When the seed pods that follow are ripe, they turn white and the seeds inside are brown or black and hard.

buttery flowers

THE MAGIC OF PRIMROSES

Folklore has it that if you grow primroses, your garden will be protected from adversity. In Germany, the goddess Perchta, who kept tabs on naughty children, lured them into her mountain hall with primroses.

COLLECT SEEDS AT THE END OF SUMMER

🧺 AUGUST TO SEPTEMBER

◆ AS SOON AS YOU HAVE COLLECTED THEM, DIRECTLY WHERE THEY ARE TO FLOWER

🌷 AS EARLY AS DECEMBER, NO LATER THAN MAY

↕🌱 10CM (4IN)

Uses A TEA OF PRIMROSE FLOWERS WAS CONSIDERED TO HELP NERVOUS DISORDERS, ESPECIALLY IF MADE FROM FRESH PETALS AND DRUNK IN THE MONTH OF MAY. A GOOD LUCK CUSTOM WAS TO HANG A WREATH OF PRIMROSES AND OTHER SPRING FLOWERS OVER THE DOOR ON MAY EVE (BELTANE), THEN LEAVE IT UNTIL IT WITHERED. PRIMROSE FLOWERS ARE EDIBLE AND HAVE A DELICATE, BUTTERY FLAVOUR. THEY CAN BE EATEN RAW OR USED IN CONSERVES, SYRUPS AND TEAS.

98 NIGELLA

(NIGELLA DAMASCENA)
★ *also known as love-in-a-mist, St Catherine's flower*

Few plants are as ethereal and delicate as nigella. Each flower's many papery petals appear to float among filigree foliage that surrounds it like a ruff. Then, once the flowers have gone, the striped, spiky seed heads appear, looking as though they have been inflated by fairies.

Uses
THE SEED HEADS LOOK GREAT IN DRIED FLOWER ARRANGEMENTS, BUT THE SEEDS ARE NOT EDIBLE — IT IS THOSE FROM *NIGELLA SATIVA* (A DIFFERENT, SIMILAR SPECIES) THAT ARE USED IN INDIAN, MIDDLE-EASTERN AND NORTH AFRICAN DISHES.

THE MAGIC OF NIGELLA
The open, many petalled flower has been compared to the wheel on which St Catherine was martyred, hence its common name of 'St Catherine's flower'.

🧺 EARLY AUTUMN, WHEN SEED HEADS ARE COMPLETELY DRY AND BROWN, BUT WILL ALSO SELF-SEED READILY

🌿 JULY TO AUGUST

↕🌱 UP TO 60CM (2FT)

 STRAIGHT AFTER COLLECTING, DIRECTLY WHERE THEY ARE TO FLOWER, IN A SUNNY SPOT

99 ECHINACEA

(ECHINACEA PURPUREA)
★ *also known as purple coneflower, hedgehog*

The purple, daisy-like flowers of this perennial plant brighten borders in late summer. The central 'cone' of the flower stands proud from the petals, giving it one of its common names 'purple coneflower'. This becomes a spiny seed head later in the year, which is why it is also called 'hedgehog'. Originally from North America, where it grows on prairies and in open woods, its roots were sucked by Indigenous Americans to treat toothache, coughs and infection. High in antioxidants, it can be bought over the counter in tablet form to head off colds and flu.

use leaves to make a tea

THE MAGIC OF ECHINACEA
Steep the flowers in oil over a low heat for 15 to 20 minutes. The resulting potion, dabbed in the corners of the house and on doors and windows, is said to protect the home.

Uses
A GARGLE MADE FROM A TINCTURE OF ECHINACEA FLOWERS CAN HELP TO SOOTHE THROAT INFECTIONS.

GATHER SEEDS WHEN THE SEED HEAD IS BROWN

🧺 OCTOBER, WHEN THE SEED HEAD IS TOTALLY BROWN

🌱 JULY TO SEPTEMBER

 UP TO 1.5M (4FT 11IN)

◆ AUGUST, SO THAT IT WILL FLOWER THE FOLLOWING YEAR

100 ⟩ BORAGE

𝖯 (BORAGO OFFICINALIS)
★ also known as starflower, ox's tongue, bee-bread, cool tankard

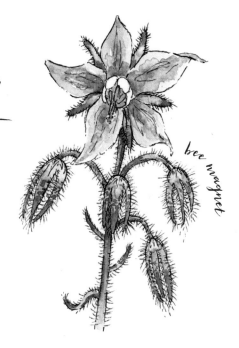
bee magnet

Borage is an annual herb but once you have grown it, you are never without it, as it self-seeds happily all over the place, withstanding all weathers. This may not be a good thing – it is a large, hairy plant that occupies a lot of space. Any ugliness, however, is mitigated by its pretty, star-shaped blue flowers that draw bees to them like a magnet. Also, the flowers can be frozen in ice-cubes to prettify summer drinks. Both the flowers and the leaves taste a little like cucumber, so are a welcome addition to a salad, and the young leaves are very high in vitamin C.

SOW SEEDS IN FULL SUN

THE MAGIC OF BORAGE
Borage has long been used in magic to bestow courage and relieve melancholy. Roman soldiers ate it before going into battle and medieval knights had it embroidered on their scarves. Culpeper, the herbalist, suggests eating its leaves 'to dispel pensiveness and melancholy' and seventeenth-century philosopher and scientist Francis Bacon said that it had 'an excellent spirit to repress the fuliginous vapour of dusky melancholie'.

Uses SOW BORAGE SEEDS IN YOUR VEGETABLE PATCH TO PROTECT BEANS, SPINACH AND BRASSICAS FROM APHIDS. YOU CAN ALSO MAKE A SOUP FROM ITS LEAVES, IF YOU ARE FEELING A LITTLE ANXIOUS AND NEED BUCKING UP.

 SEPTEMBER   JUNE TO AUGUST

 FEBRUARY OR MARCH, DIRECTLY WHERE THEY ARE TO FLOWER, IN FULL SUN   60CM (2FT)

About the author

Clare Gogerty lives on a smallholding in Herefordshire, where she grows vegetables and flowers, keeps chickens and sheep, and is gradually reintroducing the magic into her plot. Heritage apples grow in the orchard, a wildflower meadow has been sown and flowers have been allowed to self-seed and become unruly. After years of living in London, where she worked as a magazine editor, she is immersing herself in the magic, mystery and folklore of the country. Fortunately, Herefordshire is choc-a-bloc with leylines, sacred sites, soft hills and crystal-clear springs. She is a member of the Order of Bards, Druids and Ovates and pays special attention to the turning of the year and the spirit of the land.

Clare is the author of *The Witch's Yearbook: Spells, stories, tools and rituals for a year of modern magic* (David & Charles, 2021), *Sacred Places: Where to find wonder in the world* (Aster, 2020) and *Beyond the Footpath: Mindful adventures for modern pilgrims* (Piatkus, 2019), among other titles.

USEFUL BOOKS

Boxer, Arabella and Black, Philippa, *The Herb Book* (London: Book Club Associates, 1980)

Cunningham, Scott, *Cunningham's Encyclopedia of Magical Herbs* (Woodbury, MN: Llewellyn Books, 2020)

Lawrence, Sandra, *The Witch's Garden* (London: Welbeck, 2020)

Oakley Harrington, Christina, *The Treadwell's Book of Plant Magic* (London: Treadwell's Books, 2020)

Stodola, Jiri and Volak, Jan, *The Illustrated Book of Herbs* (London: Octopus, 1986)

INDEX

A DAVID AND CHARLES BOOK
© David and Charles, Ltd 2023

David and Charles is an imprint of David and Charles, Ltd
Suite A, Tourism House, Pynes Hill, Exeter, EX2 5WS

First published in the UK and USA in 2023

A catalogue record for this book is available from the British Library.

ISBN-13: 9781446309544 paperback
ISBN-13: 9781446382127 EPUB
ISBN-13: 9781446382110 PDF

This book has been printed on paper from approved suppliers and made from pulp from sustainable sources.

MIX
Paper from responsible sources
FSC
www.fsc.org   FSC® C012521

Printed in China through Asia Pacific Offset for: David and Charles, Ltd
Suite A, Tourism House, Pynes Hill, Exeter, EX2 5WS

10 9 8 7 6 5 4 3 2 1

Publishing Director: Ame Verso
Senior Commissioning Editor: Lizzie Kaye
Managing Editor: Jeni Chown
Editor: Jessica Cropper
Project Editor: Michelle Clark
Head of Design: Anna Wade
Designer and Illustrator: Prudence Rogers
Pre-press Designer: Ali Stark
Production Manager: Beverley Richardson

David and Charles publishes high-quality books on a wide range of subjects. For more information visit www.davidandcharles.com.

Follow us on Instagram by searching for @dandcbooks_wellbeing.